# An
# Attempt

DONOVAN BLAZE WALTERS

To David, Skip, Thomas and Carson.

# CONTENTS

# ACKNOWLEDGMENTS

I would like to express my very great appreciation to the following:

-Logan, for being a young, curious boy.

-Kasandra, for being a fantastic sister and whatnot.

-Ma, for being my Mom. If I had to have another Mom, I'd tell her to go kick rocks and find you. Plus, you open jars for me.

-Pops, for being my dad and stuff. Halo will always be our thing.

-Lynn, for pretty much raising me with Ma. Sorry for the mess I made that one time when I was 10.

-Lauri, for being an awesome baker and sharing your comic collection with me.

-Tim, for being a good friend. Also for not ratting me out that one time to Gunny.

-Bill, for taking me to lunch all the time and letting me play my explicit hip hop.

-Zack, for not killing me when I threw that full Gatorade bottle and it hit you in the face. You're the boss, dude.

-Kiersten, for being my spirit sister, and supporting me in literally everything I did.

-Ty-ty, for being another sister and always listening.

-Gunny, for being a badass and preparing for bootcamp.

-Major, for being a badass officer and preparing me for life.

-Biggs, for meeting up with me that one Halloween party in Bellingham. You know, the one we went to that was hosted by that one girl I had taken out and got super drunk with the year before, but then at the party she also got wasted and got all weird with her boyfriend while we were there, and then that one guy said he'd knock me out or something, and you laughed. We also got pesto pizza.

-Sean, dude, you were my partyrocker bro, and gym buddy.

-Magic, for being my brofessor. Yes, that's a term. Look it up. On Youtube. In fact, just look up BroScience.

-Every Marine I've served with, because I'm cheating. There are too many. But you all influenced my life, one way or another. I will never forget any of you.

-Mr. Garrett, for being a mentor in the ways of the Corps.

-John John, for being a badass artist and recognizing fans.

-Eric, for sharing good times and music with me.

-Sergio, for being enthusiastic about sharing both of your band's music.

-Stevo, dude, for being a great friend to me, a fellow surfer. Also thanks for saving my life that one time I got swept under the pier when we surfed that storm. I still don't know how my board survived that, unlike the bottoms of my feet. Remember how I was all bleeding from it, and I got blood in my brand new Vans? It's still there, dude! It won't come out. I tried using bleach but it didn't work. Made my shoe smell like an office toilet, though.

-Danny, for inviting me bowling and I had all that emergency gear to pull that one guy's truck off that hill along the train tracks. He was so wasted.
-Shaun, for fixing all my surfboards, multiple times. You're a great shaper.
-Brian, for being a surfer bro.
-Kody, for teaching how to surf. It changed my life.
-Cam, for being my Washingtonian dude in Pulgas.
-Robin, for being my Washingtonian dudette in Point Loma.
-Megs, for serving me all the drinks at Maloney's, for being so nice to me over such a long period of time, and letting me run Motley. And eating my food.
-Shane (the one with a Tortoise), for being a good friend and letting me pretty much live at your house and having me a part of your family. Hi, Devon!
-Shane (the one with a beard), for being hipster (ha).
-Matthew, for getting me a pack of cigarettes, even though they were for Taylor. Matt, did you see what I said about Shane? He's going to be pissed. What a hipster.
-Taylor, for being my best Marine friend in the shop.
-Michael and Kent, for being my best Marine friends.
-Katelyn and Ash, for being amazing supporters of Michael and Kent.
-Atticus and Jayden, for letting me watch you two grow up. Uncle Don misses you guys.
-Every surfer I've ever met out on the water, for helping me grow as one of you.
-David, for always remembering me, no matter how little I visited your book store in Seattle.
-Corona, for being my fellow reggae man.
-Bedolla, for being a bro.
-Jake, for keeping me honest.
-Rick, for being so damn funny.
-Momo, for watching all our movies, even the scary ones. You loco.
-Omy, for always hanging out even though Rick was an ass.
-Troy, for being a mentor and friend.
-John (good luck trying to figuring out this one), for being an amazing boss, mentor and friend.
-Tom da Bomb, for telling me how it was.
-Adam, for showing me kindness.
-Ryan, for helping me out with FSMAO, among other things.
-Andrew, for always respecting me as your boss and friend.

-Cody, for being such an outstanding Marine.

-Bowbow, you crazy dude, for being a great guy.

-TJ, for being my first and appreciative Marine.

-Raul and Andy, for being outstanding Mechs.

-Brain, for being a good friend and older brother to me. How's Florida, by the way? Are there any waves or what?

-Maynor, for showing me the Dark Side of the Force. Way past the Millennium.

-Brad, for taking care of my sister. You do great job of it.

-Matt (another good luck, there's like twenty in Chattanooga), for welcoming me in town with open arms. For also letting me enjoy your establishment, drinking all the coffee (from El Salvador, no less). I pretty much wrote more than half of my collection there.

-Natacia, for being awesome and not killing me.

-Brody, dude, for being a best friend in this crazy town, for skating with me at all times, and being a real good guy.

-Josh and Linda, for being great friends and always remembering me.

-Sadie, for being gorgeous and my primary poem editor. Someone I could always call, about anything.

-Andrea, for bringing me into the Yoga Landing family.

-Ed, for being an interesting and good friend.

-Wai, for being a friend I could depend on and actually caring about my birthday.

-Angela, for the fantastic advice.

-Patty, for being a nice and open person.

-Alexis, for being gorgeous and an amazing instructor. And for playing Sister Nancy that one Vinyasa class.

-Kaitlyn, for being a fellow spiritually sound person. Always a pleasure to take your class.

-Maggie, for challenging me and pushing me, a true teacher.

-Evan, for getting me into true longboarding.

-Drean, for teaching me what you did and getting me started on my journey to one day become a real chef. Seriously, man, thanks. Nothing but love.

-Deb, you literally made me a hundred cortados, probably more. Thanks for tolerating me. Also, please read at least this line before you use this book as a doorstop. Stop laughing. Though I guess you can if you want, because you won that one Latte Art competition against Brody. I will say, though, that I was definitely responsible for his intoxication. So, you know. Do you owe me money? Or like a macchiato? Never mind, those are gross, like some parts of California. Well. LA is ok, I mean, San Francisco is so cool, but I'm telling you, it's all about San Diego. No, as in the Mission Beach/Pacific Beach/Ocean Beach part. Parking really sucks, though. In fact, one time when I was in Mission Beach, my girlfriend had me park in this spot

CLEARLY marked red but she was all "it's fine, Donovan," and sure enough the next morning I walked her dog and we had tickets. She thought it was funny that I was wigging out and she took pictures of me. So yeah, parking can be a bit time consuming.

-Abbi, for being inquisitive and sharing your life with me. As in the baptism.

-Matte, for making me feel welcome where ever you saw me.

-Joy, for going above and beyond with editing and making me a better writer.

-Melissa, for being interested even with the giant workload of nursing school.

-Vinay, for being the happiest, strongest man I have ever met. You are who I want to be like, my friend.

-Ashley, for being the only real military haircut barber I can find and showing me so much kindness.

-Peri, for being a nice and quiet friend, always interested in what I had to say.

-Matt, for having a badass bar, being nice to new guy in town and treating me as one of your favorite patrons.

-Jeff, for making me awesome food every time I came in to write.

-Nelson, for being such a swell guy and rocking the best shaved head.

-Jason, for always having a smile and soda ready for me whenever I walked in.

-Jade, for all your fantastic editing.

-Christina, for help with format, editing, final proofing and review.

-Christina, for your absolute fantastic art. I'm honored you worked so hard for me.

-Many strangers I do not know, for so many were the subject or inspirations of my poetry.

-And last, but not least... you know who you are. Thank you for putting me on this path, for pushing me and supporting me in the art of the written word. This would have not happened if you hadn't compelled me to continue writing. I believe it was the day you were thrown into the pool at Nick's? Anyway. Thank you for every single moment we shared. I treasure every memory of us.

Every one of you influenced my poetry. You all made me the poet, and person, I am today.

Again, thank you all.

# INTRODUCTION

To be frank, I like to think of poetry as one way to communicate. Down to the tee, it can be either the heaviest, deepest, most sincere conveyance of the soul or a whimsical way to whirl words around.

I love poetry. I love how words can be twisted and made to evoke emotion and imagery. Trying to practice that, this started out as an attempt to appease someone who requested a few times over that I should write poetry, after reading some poems I had spun up while in high school.

It turned into something more.

From little poems typed and sent over text messaging to what turned into a portfolio I made online. What I wasn't expecting was the feedback. In general, very positive, some not at all. But it was there. I began writing and posting at a feverish rate. My poetry began to evolve and grow, some painting these epic images I had in my head, from love poems to inner thoughts I had during my daily life.

All these poems are in chronological order from when I posted them, namely the very first two written in 2008. Subsequent poems span from the fall of 2014 to the summer of 2015.

I hope you enjoy these pieces. I even have seven pieces, collected as 'Barely Poetry,' which all span across this sci-fi war universe I had in my head. But most are just about my life. This is more than an attempt to write poetry, it's an attempt at being an adult, at growing up. Being a man, being humble, sometimes falling. Sometimes catching a good wave, sometimes wiping out.

And sometimes, writing out a poem that hits the right notes.

"If you can walk you can dance, if you can talk you can sing."
-Zimbabwean Proverb

# 1 THIS LONELY ROAD

"It is lonely, this road, on which I trudge along.
I sometimes look up at the sky, and wonder
What is it like, to be the object of affection?
To be the one who makes her slumber with ease and security.
To be the one whom she sees when she closes her eyes.
To be the one she thinks of when she contemplates serenity.

As I march on, my destination unknown,
I instead focus on my task at hand.
For it is something woefully practiced, in the name of something
I don't yet understand.
But I can do it well, and I'm well known for it.
But can it be something I am proud of?

My brethren hold me high, for the work I have done,
and my family holds true to the lies that I live
for to be what I am is not what I once thought.

And then I think,
What of this one I dream of?
Can she bear the burden I bear, if she is to be mine?
And myself hers and only hers?

Can I bring myself to keep her awake at night,
worried about my well-being?
Can I live cognizant of her being left behind
while I wage war in a far off land?

Yes... I can,
for it is you I dream of, the one I wish to be with,
and the thing I realize, as I walk along some more,
is that you were the one
who kept me going all along.

It is cold, this road, on which I trudge along
I sometimes look up at the sky, and wonder
What is it like, to be the object of affection?
And I just remember it's you."

# 2 EYES

"How preposterous, I think to myself,
are your words coming from your mouth.
To think that I would be fooled, was I a fool,
to be played and made to act like a tool.

You seem to think that you have me read.
That I am an idiot, with all these lies you've fed.
And it pains me to think that you once were my life,
and it was you I dreamed of to call my wife.

But my beautiful, I must apologize, for I have cheated
even though you never realized it due to you being so conceited.

for I know the truth,
my beautiful,
and your deceit will no longer bear fruit.

For I can see as plain as day that you.
In fact. Are a lie.
This relationship,
to be terse, is a lie.

Our whole life together,
to be frank, was a lie.
And they leak from you as I stare into your eyes.

They say that "the eyes are the key to the soul."
like something can be fetched with a fishing pole.
But that is laughably incorrect, as is you,
because it's in fact a gateway to tell the truth.

Because I see the deceit, the hate, the conniving and manipulation,
as you think my mind is made for your verbal fornication.
And I know the one way to see what is truly you.
For that, there's only one thing I have to do.

I just have to look in your eyes,
once so beautiful to me.
But then all I see is lies,
and it's disappointing that it's all I greet."

# 3 THE LADY OCEAN

"I pull to you, and squeeze to a stop,
my heart pounding in my ears. Deafening
is your solace, the eternal push,
of your eternal ebb.

I finally breathe in, and I am awash of your scent, rather,
your breath is lapsed with my own,
the bite of the salt lapping over my tongue.
I can taste you.

I move to you, and I am ready,
like a lover moving to the bed.
Though I am no stranger, I still slow my approach,
for me, myself, am no stranger to your wrath.

I have been shoved by you before,
and your embrace can be harsh,
or as gentle as the first kiss we shared.

And again, we kiss, my skin touching your own,
and your warmth, or lack thereof,
washes over my being.

Cooling me, cleansing me anew.

You complete me. You calm me. You clean me. You are my tide, my pull.

I run into your embrace, and wield forth my weapon,
and throw myself into your open arms.

And you catch me, but not lightly,
and down I fall.
For though you hold me, your grasp is not focused.

So I, myself, must focus my will,
and push out, towards you,
towards your infinite horizon.

You become rough, and thrashing,
and I catch your protest,
my face smacks back, my breathing halts still.

And finally I break free, and mount my steed, and turn my attention unto
you.

I will not turn my back,
though as enticing as it may,
for you are the Queen, the Mother,
and the one who would throw me.

Throw me down, drown me in your embrace.

But also lift me, I think...

And so I turn, and stroke with all my love, all my strength...

And I am pushed, by your own glory and grace.

I stand, and float, and rush towards the shore. And finally, I am free.

Nothing. Else. Matters.
Time, such a fleeting subject, becomes nil.

Nothing else matters. Except our dance, our little embrace.

My body, so tense, becomes numb, and I can only feel you, giving me grace.

And so, our exchange, gone,
as fast as it came,
disappears into the sand. But my heart remains.

My love remains. Oh, Ocean!
Never have I felt this before!
For I love you, oh Ocean,
and I paddle out for more."

# 4 THE BED

"The doorknob turns, and we brush inside,
and though our minds are on one another,

our eyes lead in, away from each other,
unto the corner, so soft,
softly aglow.

Our giggles permeate the silence,
softly, gently,
and we both look back,
the door shutting us from the world.

But that is just fine,
for our world is over there...
in that corner. So big, is this land!

First you, such a beau, crawl onto its tracks, and the sheets bend with your
movement, and I,

well. Await for you to gaze back.
Such anticipation!

And I cannot wait any longer.
I pounce. But ever so gently,
for this land of ours,
is encompassing of what we are feeling this night.

So soft, its embrace, and soon ours is too,
but warm, for your skin is against mine.

And now, our lips, for surely time is no more, are locked in an unspoken
dance. Coy passion,
so vexing, plays along our tongues.

But this is reserved, for this new found destination,
and only limited, by the edge of the bed.

Shall I keep going? No. But why?
Because our vibes are augmented,
by the sheets and pillows of the bed.

The night, so short, lasts an eternity,
for sure, for our bodies meld,
our hearts purr, and we make love unto the other... on this soft bed.

But the fact remains, so quickly,
when the sun creeps into the room,
and your stilled slumber is present next to my own,

that these moments, so fleeting,
thankfully last forever.

Because our love is only begun,
in this soft bed of yours..."

# 5 THE SCULPTOR'S MECCA

"Into the hollowed grounds, I step,
but not lightly. This is different.
I am not here for my usual stroll,
my face does not have my soft smile.

Instead, my pace is set, and its speed not slow,
There is work to be done here.
I have sweat to put into these halls.

I plug in, but it's with such a joy,
And I quench my thirst, with a source so rejuvenating,
A different smile smears itself onto my face.

I am here, my mecca,
My holy ground.
This place, I am only me.
I have no enemy but myself.
And I am my own greatest obstacle.

There is no love, to attract my attention,
there is no wind, to break my focus,
and there is no worry that encompasses my mind.

Only one thing remains, and it's solely my physical being.
My one and only being, my own shrine.

And so! Like a sculptor, I seize the hammer!

And I STRIKE at the stone!

And I HEAVE the handle!

And I breathe in the dust that settles.
Such heat,
that is exhausted from the skin.
Such heat!

I am now in motion, mindless,
but with such focus,
my conscious is gone,
and my stone becomes hewed.

I chip, and strike, and crack into the block,
and within the block I see and make,
A MONUMENT!

This, glory by me, is me!
The own work of my source of strife,
given unto me by my own hand.
Aren't I entitled to the sweat of my brow?

NO, says the world;
NO, says the hungry hand;
NO, says the ones who need me.

But they cannot be heard,
the noise is too loud.
I focus,
and it becomes louder!

I strike! I strike with my hammer!
Unto the chisel held by my left,
I let a grunt escape from my lips,
and I strike with my right!

And I let go.

I step back,
and glare at my block.
So little progress, it seems.
But so much work!

And I see my own reflection,
and see the block
that is seen by others,
and I see what they see.

This piece of art,
this unfinished sculpture,
I have no sense of completion.
I cannot stop.

So I leave, this temple,
where so many other stone workers, and masons, and carpenters,
come to work their medium,
and complete their own monument.

We all come,
we all see,
that we are all working,
but on our own works.

I am my own obstacle,
but my own salvation,
my own friend.
And I smile.

And so I leave, these hollowed grounds,
with the determination of yesterday,
and the dedication of today,
to have the motivation of tomorrow,

to return.

For I am not finished,
a sculpture still hungry,
for the final product in his imagination.

I will return,
and I will sculpt,
and I will build,
this monument of physical perfection."

# 6 THE CELL

"And so, alas, my arrival is known,
though sooner I'd rather hide my face,
and run the news aground.

Alas, my last, final breathe,
of the sea green sky,
is finished. And I am left,
to my own devices.

In my own prison. My cell,
so small, encompasses me,
and squeezes light out.

Alas, my load is dropped,
and my skin, burning as such,
must be cleansed. It burns!

The basin! The water!
It flows, but not warm,
for these shrunken halls hold no remorse,
for weary and tired.

Yet I must sleep. And eat.
And I digress.

I cleanse the burning, and come back anew,
and thus begin to lose my urge
to sulk.

This is my home! These small, littered walls. And though they aren't mine,
I am theirs.

I slumber in this rack,
I cleanse in this sink,
I eat in this chair,
I dream,

staring at these walls.

I see castles, and knights!
Storming across a plain to war.
I see monsters and beasts!
Lashing out for purchase.

I see ships that fly and cars that glide,
and people who conquer the sea.

But in one little spot,
where my reflection is shown,
I see a man,
who looks back at me.

And this man, in these walls,
remembers to thank,
the ones who shared this cell.

For it's because of people like me,
and people like them,
that others
sleep so well.

And so I shall too,
with love in my heart,
though it belongs to someone not here.

But that is just fine, and I fall in my own bed,
and again...
stare at these walls."

# 7 NOTHING BUT TIME

"The clock ticks by.
The minutes seem to fly.
The seconds crawl away.

Why! How is this so,
how is this possible?
This phenomenon, this joke,
of my concept of time,

is intangible, like time,
but accountable as the hour,
and I dive deep into my mind,
reaching to grasp time.

It hurts, my head throbs,
but I can count the seconds
between each wave of pain.

Breathtaking!
Breathe.

Time is just crawling by.

I think of the time, one time,
when our lips first met,
and that moment of time,
ground to a halt.

And the night blurred,
and the streets quieted down,
and the people disappeared,
and it was just our kiss.

Lasting a second.
Lasting forever,

in my mind. That one time.

On contrary! Our new beginning,
the days that have passed since,
have blurred, too fast!
You can barely make out the details.

Every one I remember. The slow of the seconds, as my fingers run
through your hair,

The crawl of the minute,
as our fingers intertwined,
and the hours that would pass impossibly quick,
as our bodies became one.

What a joke, this time,
the time we spend apart,
is like a melting statue,
being pulled apart by not heat, nor man, but eons of time.

It crawls, too slow,
it digresses left and right.

But then the time
will come,
and our lips will reunite,
and then time will fast-forward,
and it will be time to leave again.

And then I will watch time slow,
and then it will drift by my eyes,
too fast to comprehend.
Romantic. Truly.

Nothing but time,
indeed."

# 8 THE TITAN'S WASH

"The deed is done,
the battle is won,
and I, a machine,
am burning hot.

Time to turn off the engine,
let the fires burn low,
turn all the right cranks
let the gears spin slow.

Slowly I grudge along
to my own maintenance bay.
And with a careless subconscious,
turn the wrench that sprays.

Down goes the grime,
washed from my metal,
and the steam sears off me,
as the water clashes with my heat.

So good does it feel,
be it curious, this machine feels,
that the oil, and dirt, and rust,
be busted from my wheels.

My pistons slacken,
my hydraulics whine down,
my actuators stop turning,
and my engine stops its sound.

The wash! So good,
and now the scrubbing begins,
and the sweet smelling solvent,
Turns all my shell to sheen.

My giant structure shudders,
as I am washed anew,
and my small bay space
is filled with a mesmerizing brew.

But this, these suds, wash down,
the massive dirt collecting drain,
for all the war machines do as I,
and our war models, we maintain.

And so, I come out,
and my engine fires are relit bright,
and my metal is made dry,
and its paint is all that shines.

The fire is hot!
My engine burns clean!
The gears are again spinning,
and so forth goes this machine."

# 9 THE VENUE

"The heat, so intense,
packed shoulder to shoulder,
wafts over me,
and my brow perspires.

Who are all these people?
Are they here for the same reason?
Will they understand the rhyme?
Will they get the soul?

These thoughts distract me
from the noisy, indistinguishable chatter,
and my own thoughts, all too alone,
fill my head up as I wait.

For I am alone,
no one would come.
No one would see the show
of my own little world.

But no matter! Does it matter?
I realize I'm surrounded by people like me,
they must be like me, since they're here at midnight,
waiting for the first drum kick.

Soon the stage lights glare, and swell the stage,
and all around me people push,
against the front of this cage,

only eighty folks allowed, in this
small ass place,
but about a hundred other hip-hop heads
crowd the mic and the table.

They finally walk in! I barely know their names,
but the crowd cheers on, and my voice is now found,
and this crew strolls ups,
and the mic blares out

"Mix the beat, my man, let's show them why they came out."

And the funky beat fills the space,
my ears whine with the intense volume,

But the lyrics! So cool,
I eat it up like a spoiled brat.
His words hit me,
And the words have meaning.

And I thank the chance that I have, to come and see this group,
in the too cramped venue,
that they probably could barely book.

But I enjoy this moment,
surrounded by faces that I don't even know,
because I'm with people like me,
the ones who came for the show."

# 10 HIS APPROACH

"The room is COLD.
But the room is dark,
I like.
The bed is warm,
and so is this comforter.

Mmm. I love to sleep in.
Though my eyes are closed,
I see my room, for I know it well.
And my palace I lay in,
is meant for my slumber.

Yet I hear that sound,
Oh, how I detest so!
That nasty mongrel,
always disturbing my sleep.
I hate him.

But it is quickly hushed,
and the front door creaks.
What time is it?
Who cares! So quick!

It's not bright out,
I muffle out a protest,
and pull my sheets closer.

Movement outside moves,
and I can feel it move to me,
and then my room is exposed.
Though I cannot see,

I know it's him.
He's here!

I don't even turn, there's no real need. I just listen, and smile,
at his soft cooing of my name.

I hear him peel off his layers,
they're pesky, and get in the way,
and they pile on my floor,
before he crawls onto my bed.

And at first I feel, his soft fingers touch,
I let him know I like it,
as my shoulder shudders through.

His arms try to wrap around me,
as he shoves his legs down the sheets,
he moves his body close to mine,
and our cuddle becomes complete.

I turn my head back, and soon together are our lips,
and he plays nice, for in my ear,
instead of tongue, words,
escape his lips;

'I love you, mi amor,'
and I snuggle deep into his arms.
For this Sunday morning, he promised,
we're going to just sleep in,
and he's all that I need to be warm."

*This poem was written from her point of view, observing me.*

# 11 THE TRACKER

"And now I prowl,
like the prey I track,
as it prowls, fuming,
along the jungle river bank.

The tall weeds hide me,
and thankfully so,
for I am a hunter,
ever so hungry for this trophy.

The striped beast, a hunter itself,
magnificent beyond others,
paws the running water, perhaps
frustrated with its unlucky fortune.

But no matter, for at this moment,
the tiger is still, and so I know
to take this shot, as the opportunity is so fleeting.

What a creature! I try to savor the moment,
before my weapon goes off,
and makes this scene change irrevocably.

The heat, once withering, is now a calm comparison,
and it brings waves among the trees,
of moisture in the air.

The chatter of the jungle,
full of animals and critters,
alive with elated sounds
and its own moving vibe.

The scent of sweet flowers,
sliced clean with the water,
and the old, wise smell,
of the clay river bank.

And the sky, so glorious!
So large is its scene,
as the large sun sets,
in this jungle I now occupy.

And so I ready,
this scene forever locked away,
as a memory I will cherish,
on this hunt for this tiger.

I bring the rubber to my eye
of the optical for accuracy,
and focus my zoom,
to line up the shot.

The beast, in my lens, looks right at me,
and my heart quickens,
as I slowly squeeze the apparatus,
to make this whole thing go off.

I shoot the tiger, and it turns,
and bounds for its life.
I missed!
I line up another shot.

I shoot again, this time, the shot was very clean,
but before I could finish the job,
the beast was across the river.
The thrill of the hunt! No matter the outcome,

what a moment!
To bring such joy, and knowledge to others,
of these wondrous beasts,
to the young and yearning masses.

To bring it to museums, and magazines, is my goal,
and the whole experience,
full circle,
makes the jungle so worth it.

Still, quite a great shot,
I must go for another!

And so, I prowl,
after the one who prowls,
because I need to shoot it again,
and get that perfect shot.

But before that, with care,
for I do not want my efforts go to waste,
I take my unnecessarily expensive DSLR camera,
and put it in its case."

*Read this poem twice.*

# 12 THE CONVULSION

"The wind whispers
into my ear; such hatred!
No amount of tugging at
the collar of my cloak
can quiet its lewd cursing.

I struggle up the hill,
placing one foot in front of the other,
and this dark and stormy night
shows no interest in watching me succeed.

This damnable weather! And
not a star in sight!
The Moon, unreliable, is absent
of course. The one time I wish
to see its soft gaze set aglow my path.

The tree branches rustle, as the leaves have begun to die,
and adds to this eerie scene,
with nothing less than an additional
distracting sound.

The blustery wind sweeps up and down
the path, rushing creatures at my feet to devour me,
only to find them to be forest debris,
and they crash into my feet.

I trudge, with little hope
of my ordeal to soon be over,
and just as I begin to despair,
a light in the distance,
makes its impromptu entrance!

Oh, that light! That blessed, blessed beacon,
my pace quickens,
first of my heart, then of my gait,

with the strong determination
to be encased in the glow ahead.

As the light becomes closer, it begins taking shape,
the outline of a lantern,
swaying from a hand.

Wait.

Why is there a lantern at this hour,
with no one to hold it?

There is no one grasping its handle,
and yet it approaches me!

I turn, quickly, and start to walk back
from whence I came,

but the light, now, becomes brighter,
as if the nonexistent walker
has doubled his pace!

I begin to run, this time with more gusto,
and now I hear the lantern behind me,
dangling by my head,
its rung squeaking against the metal,
the latch unhinged, the glass swinging open!

Shrill, as I run, is the sound that I notice, with no help
from the wind,
rushing by my ears!

Fear, coursing through my veins,
fuels me beyond my limits, surprising even me as I zip down the path,

and as soon as I begin to find comfort in some distance,
by foot finds unwanted purchase on a root!

I fly, and look, and the light is bright from behind,
and I watch my own shadow grow,
as I plummet straight into the dirt,

I hit, hard, and I hear the lantern
do so as well,
glass shattering, along with my wrists,
and now pain shoots up my arms,
and screams at my brain.

I cry out, and turn around,
and gasp.

Gasping awake. In my bed.
In this room.

I am sweating. I sigh, and breathe out,
to slow my heartbeat.
What a dream! Ha.

I get up, and go to the hallway, so dark,
to enter the restroom for the gla-

and freeze.

Why is there a glass broken on my floor? Odd. I had left a glass full of
water in the restroom.

I look at the door. I had locked it before I went to bed.
It's wide open.

Adjoining, the closet door is ajar.
Odd. It was shut earlier.

The light snaps on in the closet.
Strange.
It can only be turned on
from the inside.

A shadow moves-"

# 13 TOURNAMENT

"One step closer,
I bring my suit up to bear,
my shield up high,
barely able to see past my visor.

My opposite, my black,
my muse, myself.
The other knight, down
the mud-pocked track,

awaits
to charge at me.
To lay waste to me.
To kill.

And I the same!
Yet I cannot jest!
The fear coursing through my veins
is arcing stuff.

What? Are you kidding?
Stuff?
All thoughts sprawl out
and twirl in my head,

pierced only by the drum gongs in my ears.
If I was lesser, I would falter.
I would shake.
But I grab the reins and stomp my steed up to the mouth of the track.

I could die!
I could be impaled!
Goodness, his joust looks more like a great pike with every stride!

But I am a knight. A gentleman!
I swear on my name to fight,
for those who cannot. I must be brave.

I must have courage.
For indeed I am scared. But that is okay.
Courage allows one to proceed in the face of danger!
With calmness and firmness!

And so I ride,
my heart stopped,
my joust lowered,
My whole life in this,

I smash ahead, and see I had one
outcome to really worry about.
Looking past the foe,
to the maiden in the crowd. Her decision?

She declined! Was not my joust enough to evoke her wrath?

A strong woman, for a strong man. Time will help. My helmet forgotten on
the dirt,

and my insatiable appetite only calmed by her hungry lips.

The joust over, I ready for the bout."

# 14 NIGHT SURF

"The sun sets,
and no moment too soon.
It is hardly believable
the blistering heat it brings.

And yet the night has not cooled,
and the beasts still run hot,
for the waves hit me hard,
and seemingly harder with no illumination.

My brow is creased,
and sweat runs along it,
with my lips in a snarl,
my breathe runs hot.

Hot with exhaustion,
for the heat has made me lethargic.

Hot with frustration,
for the seemingly unnecessary state of my misery.

Hot. Heat. Anger.
It runs tonight.

There is nowhere to go,
there is nowhere to dip in
and drop degrees. Just lay on
top of your sheets and sweat!

I disagree! I do not want to abide.
That is just laying down and taking the heat.

So I grab my buster, my blade,
my fantastic greatsword,
and make my way to the arena to fight.

I am armored
with nothing, not even a suit for show,
but that suit is only for warmth,
and warmth is not welcome.

Instead I embrace the cold, as it washes over me,
and cools my body,
my mood and my frown.

I run to the fight, and bring my long blade to bear,
and the beast, unseen!
Strikes at me, my face.

I am pushed back, but my determination runs hot,
and I bring the blade up,
and then down.

And now, I glide, and all the heat is forgotten.

Just the cool, unseen sensation of that feeling,
surrounded in darkness,
nothing but the Moon
illuminating the Sea.

The Moon!
So forgotten. She is like
the Ocean, in many ways. But
much more quaint. Quiet.

But just as mesmerizing.

I ride the wave, I do battle with an unseen beast,
and now I am freezing.

Ah. Now, for a warm shower!"

# 15 THAT LAST NIGHT, OR, CONSTELLATIONS WE DREW

"The darkness is overwhelming,
just another night,
and I had to go.
I had to leave your side.

But that fact was pushed aside,
as you laid on your back,
your eyes closed,
your lips slightly parted,

letting just the softest sounds
escape. Your little signs of
pure relaxation,
of my hands.

I rubbed you down,
first starting at your shoulders,
your skin kissed cold from the fan,
and brought shudders down your arm,
as my fingers traced down to your own.

You drew my other hand close and squeezed,
as the guitar quietly played next to us,
and a man sang to us, for us,
singing about drawing his own constellations.

What a song. What a perfect moment
in time.

It was getting late,
but nothing was stopping this feeling that I had,
and I could feel you felt the same way.

The way we talked,
the plans we drew up,
It was small and little and no big
decision, but you made them with me.

Such a young relationship,
slowly blossoming, still much to grow,
but the petals slowly move to uncover
the beauty that is our love.

I rub you, my palm flat against the life inside,
and you don't even move, barely breathe,

just a removed situation from such a heavy circumstance,
and we were there, not even budging. Beautiful.

I withdraw my hand,
and slowly move off. Not to hurry off,
but begrudgingly make my way to the door,
to that coffee shop,

with the sun setting on the beach,
and you lying in bed, thinking of who knew,

But what I knew, is how I will never forget every single detail
of that night.

The way the air smelled.
The way you kissed me.
The things you whispered.
The love we confessed.

And how that night,
we drew our own constellation."

# 16 ROLL, YOUNG BUCK

"Sipping on this cup,
and the mood is smooth.
But not what you expect,
this cup is just as rough

as the tunes spewing
out the speakers.

The sun litters the room through the lazily shut blinds,
and expose the smoke still dancing in the air.

With the coffee on my tongue,
I'm feeling cool. Way cool,
my main man in the chair next to me,
blowing, exhaling, us two breaking the rules,

like cool kids, bad boys,
the music pushing my mindset into frame,
on the same day I was just driving home how I've made change.

No matter, nothing matters,
for I'm too cool,
smoking with cigarettes and sipping joe,

though I know it's got too much
creamer
to make me cool.

Mad, uncomfortable, the taste is
way too plain, and I'm not cool enough
for that nonsense. What?

Call the cops, tell on me,
I'm on some nonsense,
just bounce, rock, roll, skate.

I push between one room and the next,
cigarette hanging from my lips,
orange cup in hand,

steaming with my cool coffee bean,
and this silly time in my life
I look back at and just laugh.

My goodness, what in the world
was I doing? I was ridiculous at 18.

Coffee is much better at 23.
More dignified.

Ha."

*A reflection of being a "cool kid" five years before, written as though I was 18 again.*

# 17 MY COUNTRY BAR

"Here I sit,
in this lonely country bar,
alone with my whiskey,
the sour mash on my lips.

The scene is serene,
the bar littered with few men,
cowboy hats and all.
Peanut shells litter the ground.

Here I sit,
with a love song in my heart.
The speakers play that twang,
and it speaks to the hearts of the room.

Here a man is talking with a coworker,
nursing his sorrows with a tall cool draft.
There a man stares at the wall, alone in his thoughts.

Such a moment like this I always enjoy.
Here we sit,
all here for our own reasons,
the bartender leaning over the wood,
eyes on the neon across the bar.

Slowly waltzing,
a couple hold each other,
their boots methodically, gracefully,
making a path up and down the wooden floor.

Imagine,
how many boots stomped and kicked,
how many smiles were shared,
skirts were twirled,
kisses were shared,

while the flannels were red,
the beer was cold,
the plastic cups full,
and the country tunes lit the floor up.

But not tonight.

I sit and wait,
because even though I know this scene,
and even though I can describe it,
and even though I can feel the night before in the wood below,

here I sit,
and sigh.

I do not belong here.
I am not captured by the southern girls love,
I am not drawn to that long dirt road,
and I will never own a truck.

Yes, the culture is alive,
and nice, and glorious,
but I do not belong.

I belong on the Ocean,
my ears meant to be wet
instead of ringing with the latest tunes,

I belong on the sandy beach,
tickling four strings instead of six,
cooing reggae tunes instead of southern blues,

I belong on the concrete,
the tall buildings towering over me,
the shoes and boots traded for sandals.

But I am in love,
so here I sit,
patiently waiting in this country bar,
for my love and her friend to finish their waltz,

until I can put down this glass of whiskey and pick up that bar of wax,

take this cowboy hat off and pull on my beanie,

and jamming reggae music,
around the clock.

It leaks into this country bar,
and in my head the dancehall erects,

and I smile,
a man and his thoughts,
here I sit."

# 18 DOUBT

"What a powerful force,
the unseen force,
that can force you into submission.
Effortlessly.

You can put so much effort
into something so forlorn,
something so sought out,
and then question yourself.

It makes the brave falter,
the curious hesitate,
the shy, shy away
into their own quiet minds.

It is brought upon us sometimes often,
but can catch us by surprise,
it can change your mind for you,
or make a decision in your stead.

How dare this, you may say,
but we all are victim
to this enemy on the inside,
this normal human feeling.

It isn't always bad,
for it can bring things into perspective,
show the situation and its faults
and the easy way of commencement.

But hear me now, reader,
and if nothing else from me
take heed of my next words
as they have set me free:

'Fear not the doubt that brings you to your knees,
fear not the fear of failure and all that it may bring,
because if it's worth it, you'll know it, and no matter the event,

don't give up, don't give in,
keep fighting,
and when you can, sing.'

This may seem trivial, for some situations are so dire
that a simple song is incredulous of the things we sometimes feel.

But I promise from my heart,
no matter what your tune you play,
sing out that favorite lyric,
and wash the doubt away.

When the world gets me down,
I can rely on that sound,

just sing the doubt away."

# 19 THE LIFEGUARD

"When we have no grip on reality,
and we sink into the abyss.
Inside our minds, so deep, we can become lost,
and not be seen for some time.

And in these times we will lose
all remaining remnants of what we can be, what we are,
and this is dangerous.
Despair is crushing.

But! Let us not forget,
that those who are lost can be found,
and they are those who are out at sea,
ready to dive in and pull you ashore.

I am that man, that lifeguard,
that guardian that you need.
I am one with the waves, and swimmingly I dive,
for I will swim until my heart gives out,
for you.

You may be in rough water,
being tossed around, your mind
making the water choppy,
but I will not stop until I have found you.

Your waves may be harsh on me,
other men would get out,
but not me. No! I love the Ocean,
and all its fury.

And so, I dive, and I swim,
and I see you in the distance,
not drowning, not dying,
but you are lost,
and I am here to find you.

But you ask, why?
Why do you come for me?

Why do you put yourself through this storm,
and fight the raging sea,
for me?

Because I myself was lost,
and I had no one to swim for,
no one swam for me.

I was lost, but I found myself,
and only with luck,
did I come across this love
for the Ocean.

So don't you fret, don't cry,
because I am willing to die
trying to get to you,
and though I may be thrown
against the bottom of the reef...

you're worth it."

# 20 THE MIGHTY

"The beginning of the journey
starts insignificantly,
as the seed is planted,
by some unknown fate.

Maybe by the storm, blowing the seed off the branch,
and it was swallowed by the Earth,
to be nurtured henceforth.

Or maybe by the beast,
the fruit, having the seed inside,
was the vessel that was swallowed,
and by and by found another opportunity to grow.

Or maybe by man,
who so capable of destruction,
bore a different hand, this one green,
and planted the seed with care.

No matter the method,
the seed slowly grows,
like an immovable, small child,
it sprouts ever so slightly.

The young tree is me,
having watched my leaves turn colors,
right before the very eyes
of the youth who turned adult.

A small amount
of time has crept by for me,
yet the ones who cared for me
have since left my side.

But I do not fret,
I've seen beautiful people be born,
and watch them be the parent they want to be.
Generations come and go.

And so,
I grow,
a tree turned massive,
I am mighty.

The problem with that is I see the ones I love pass.
They bring joy to only my heart,
my vibe,
my soul.

So here I am, centuries years old,
having watched over this little grave I'm here to stand guard.

That is my life.
I shall wear no crown.
I shall hold no lands.
I shall win no glory.

But no matter. I am infinite.
I am eternal."

# 21 MIDNIGHT ALARM

"You cry, and I hear.
I rise, slowly, unaware of the time.
But that isn't important.
Your body shakes with your cries.

Hush! No need to cry.
These words I do not pronounce with annoyance,
rather, with love.

As though I'm teaching you something you'll hold onto forever.

I come to you, and you cry.
You do not acknowledge my presence;
but I know you know. I am here.

I slowly take hold of you, and pick you up.
I attend to you,
though your cries do not lessen...

You are fed, and changed,
Whatever is the matter, little one?
To be frustrated with you is to be weak,
and you don't need that in your life.

What you need is love,
and I can show you that.
Give you that.

You have your whole life ahead of you,
and I can show you what I know.

Gosh, where to start! So many of my own life lessons cloud my head,
and I don't know which to teach,
but I look down at your soft eyes,
and your cries have lessened.

So I hold you close, and coo,
and sing to you, sweet child,
as I have dreamed about doing since before you were born.

I sing to you,
about the pouring rain,
I sing to you,
about the sun that shines,
just like I practiced alone,
your mother catching me in the doorway.

I sing to you,
about the green grass and how it grows.
I sing like I mean it,

and coo to you how I love you.
Love is what life costs.
And I am sure to teach you this.

Asleep in my arms,
I lay you down,
and slowly creep back to the bed,
wiping a tear from my eye,

as I praise the most high,
just to be alive.
And give thanks for you, and her,
and how much I love my life."

# 22 SELFLESSNESS

"My eyelids are so heavy,
wanting nothing more than to close.
But I cannot, for there is
too much to do.

I want to sleep,
I want to rest my bones.
These tired old bones,
which aren't so old,
ache like they are indeed.

But I have much to make happen.

The hour isn't late,
but the sun has set.
I do not want to be awake anymore,
I want to succumb to the sweet embrace of slumber,
and all its consequences.

But I will not.

I rise,
to do what must be done.
I take the needle in my hand,
and watch it dive through the cloth,
and pull it through again.

And as I rub my eyes,
for they burn so,
I watch the needle and the thread,
snake their way through my uniform,
my cloth,
my armor that I have worn, and earned, and mended so many times.

I will not sleep, and be weak.
I must render my cloth fixed,
I must pull this tear back together,
I must mend this selfless person,
and help myself.

I, annoyingly, have such an affinity
for being the one others need,
with no idea I am in need myself.

The ones who I spend the most time being there for,
first cry nay,
and then tell me I myself must attend to thee.

I will be lonely,
they point out,
but so what?
I do not care,
I do not mind.

I am the one who must be there, for others
the one fixed point,
the calm in the storm.

Alone,
I attend to me,
with a smile on my lips,
in realization they are right.

And I'll sleep later, anyway."

# 23 THE VEIL

"Ah, darling.
So beautiful, are you.
Shrouded by so much.
But it is plain to see.

If only with eyes that wish it,
to melt the veil away,
and see the beauty inside.

Your hair, you call short,
but I, I see your crown!
And unkempt it grows points,
adorned with jewels,
in the right light.

Your eyes, you call dark,
but I see them so crisp!
They do not belie your years
but relay your wisdom,
and the life you have lived.

Your smile, you call broken,
but I see fresh snow!
So bright, and genuine,
that smile that melts my heart.

Your beauty is mesmerizing,
and I know I am not
the only one who sees.

But when you look upon yourself,
you see nothing of this beauty
I pour my heart out describing.

The veil, it is thick!
But whom is to blame?
The one who pulls this over our eyes,
like a thief in disguise.

But this is no stranger,
for we are all slightly blind.
And I, too, am no exception.
For I see no man!

I see many needed corrections,
laughably far from perfection,
and can grumble all day on my flaws.

But you lift me up, with your voice,
and speak reason and praise,
to my ways and efforts and
make me pause.

Indeed! I have worked and made do,
and paid the due for what I have become.
And I have sculpted, in the Mecca,
at the hearth like Hephaestus,
and you show me I am indeed a work of art.

Like you!
So beautiful.

You have taught me to pull back this veil,
and so I say, unto you,
Darling. You are gorgeous,
see what I see.

For you make my knees weak,
with what, on the outside, I see.

But, truly, you make me melt,
with all that inner beauty."

# 24 WORDSMITH

"Sometimes, when I am alone,
it is impossible to relay what I feel.
There is no one to listen,
the others won't grasp my voice.

I, affluent, have a disposable way
that I throw out words. But again,
I laugh,
for not a letter is wasted.

I spin myself into my own twists,
the paintbrush dragged across the canvas,
my brush, my language,
my surface, your mind,
my medium, your imagination.

I can make trees peel their roots
from out the ground,
I can have giant beasts spring out of lakes,
too big to conceive how it was in such a small amount of water.

I can have the sky turn green,
and the grass turn red,
and the Ocean turn yellow.

I take my heated metal and bang against it,
like a smith working a blade,
and I smash down with my hammer,
and breathe life into a lifeless thing.

This is my skill, my unused skill,
something I love to never do.

I am wordsmith.

I make our minds come alive. But,
there is a cost,
being that the mind is fickle!

It can be put into gear, and sprung into life,
and everything I want it to do,
I can make it to be, flowing out my imagery.

But not all minds are so attuned,
with no desire to be switched to a different channel.

Of this, often, I am reminded.
And inspired, I find myself less often.

But not today.

There are those who love the written word!
There are those who yearn for the paintbrush,
and paint their canvas as well.

We, together, evoke emotion in our own ways, and that is the gift.

So I turn to my scabbard,
and unsheathe my blade,
and stab at the paper,
and write my words.

Wordsmith. I am inspired again."

## 25 SUNDAY

"The stars were out that night,
and as the conversation flowed,
so did the feeling that was growing inside.
Oh, how I love the rush.

But! To be ecstatic over the monotony of sound
that is your voice, is to be blind,
for only a fool drools over what is just
your cry.

You tell where these vibes are going,
and where we're going tonight,
and I tell you we're just getting started,
and that the feeling is just right.

Said, you're my love, my empress love,
and don't you know that you're my fire,
you're scent is what I admire,
and everything that falls though your lips I catch.

Simply, I got a fallen star,
buried deep inside of me,
and every time you're by my side,
I can't help but find myself staring in your eyes.

I never want to grow apart,
for when you're holding on my hand
you're really holding on my heart.
My heart belongs to you, and only you.

So where do we go from here? I speak as though
we have been together forever, yet,
we haven't spent more time than
the words have left that air.

I am scared, to be honest,
to jump into this with you. But I will not stop!
Fear will not rule me this day,
and I will run to the end of days to see.

What will I see?
Why,
where we end up!
With your lips on mine.

Take my hand, loved one,
and together we can jump.
I'm all over the place like this memory,
and today we will run into the sun."

## 26 OUR PATHS

"My heart is indescribable,
I don't know where to start,
with how to begin to relay
the twist that pulls it apart.

I can't stop my tears,
I can't steady my breathe,
I can't stay my hands still,
after your side I had left.

My love, I loved you,
and I still believe you loved me, too,
but life says otherwise, and you
tell me the truth, no lies.

The truth, I need to hear,
and heed the pain I caused.

My love, I was selfish,
with keeping you only to me,
and it wasn't infidelity; rather,
your love for me,
that grew us apart.

There is no lack of love! I know this,
because you have already wowed me
with what you are willing to do
for us.

For me.

And so, I must dry these tears,
for we are not mortal enemies!
We are visionaries, our new paths set in front of us,

where once our paths were one,
now this bumpy road has split into two, and so quickly have they spread.

As we walked down, our hands held tight, until
we could no longer clutch the other.

And at first, despair wrought over me.

But no more!

Our paths will intertwine again,
Though I may no longer be on your path,
I can watch you walk, and cheer,
and yell at the top of my lungs and tell the world,
Yes! Go! Run!

With new fervor,
I turn down to my path, its long winding flow ebbs over the horizon,
and out of sight, of your mind.

Let us run, and see exactly when we cross paths again!

I'll meet you at the junction."

# 27 THE GOODBYE

"The warrior leaves,
sword and shield bound upon his back,
the crest adorned on the arms
shrink into the distance from the eyes of his lover.

She holds back tears, but they fall,
and with no remorse she watches him leave.

He does not look back.

She begs silently that he turns,
just one more time,
but then dashes those yearnings,
for it will just make it that much harder.

The goodbye was almost not real,
though the night before was rough enough,
and seeing him one last time
almost seemed a mistake.

But to never really say goodbye would have been devastating,
and she was glad she asked for one more encounter.

Blessed, be he!
For going off to far off lands.

Blessed, be she!
For loving him so.

And silently she cries,
confident he can't hear her,
letting the sobs slowly roll out of her throat.
The moment was taking too long.

She looks up, and inhales-
he turns!
Making his way back,
she is stoned in her position.

Floored, figuratively,
her head spins.
She wants to run to him,
but she can't trudge forward,
her feet impossible to break from the ground.

And she smiles,
and the tears continue to fall.
But not with sadness,
but joy for another moment with him!

He approaches, still a distance away,
and suddenly her head is rushed,
swaying to and fro,
and she falls forward,

only to catch herself with a step.
And another.
And she runs!

Runs into to his arms,
for one last goodbye.

One more embrace.
One more longing look.

She sighs.

'Just go already!' she laughs out,
though they both know it's forced.

And so he does,
this time beyond the horizon,
and this time she doesn't cry.

So she waits.
And for what, she is not sure."

# 28 THE FIRST LIGHT

"The first time that we draw air,
and from what we aren't presently aware,
the cries are heard by many.

It may not always be music,
unto selfish ears,
but to this certain occasion,
it assuredly is.

The life that draws its first breathe,
in a room full of those who breath deep,
and gasp out a plethora of emotions in the instance,

is a beautiful life. Such a beautiful moment in time,
rivaled by little, perhaps nothing. And much yet to pass.

The first moment,
that the Lady, so loved,
holds the newly minted love,
the affection in the room swells against the walls.

The moment the lips of Lord and Lady press gently against the forehead,
the room spins with joy.

And so it should! For bringing
love into this world is one of
most rewarding experiences,
even if unintentional.

Sometimes the unplanned pan out,
and the best of times are times not brooded over,
and such moments in time,
however stalled,
become fleeting.

And just like the first light of the morning,
with the sun shining on our face,
the new beginnings of the day.

With all its expectations,
and hopeful bringing,

the first time a life becomes a life,

certainly coincides with the lives that bear it.

Rejoice! And praise to the most high,

the life, and all the lives that it brings together,
have just began,

like the first light that burst through the horizon,
and dances across the land,
to lavish it anew."

# 29 THE CITY LIGHTS

"Here, I lie, on my back,
furious with my own misery.
I cannot help but fume
at my own fate.

For the COLD!
So biting,
sinks its teeth into me
this one last trip to the sands.

I am a tide warrior,
a seeker of the coast,
but the sand beneath my feet this time is not of my beloved Ocean.

It is of the desert,
and though others have a true love for its inner beauty,
a beauty even I appreciate,
I have nothing but contempt for it.

However,

the roots of my deep-rooted distaste feeds from my own origins,
and where many lived and grew in lands with trees and hills,
I grew where the concrete broods,
where the cracks of the sidewalk, the only reprise
for what many saw as weeds,

I saw as flowers grow.

These nights with the City's lights setting the tone of my sleepy town,
running amuck with no supervision,
and when we'd look up,
we'd cheer at the clouds and our own stars,

The City lights!

And now, as I lie, I have grown.

For THIS place, reasons learned later,
hold for me, true lights.

Up in the sky, just absolute love,
lights, burst down unto me.
I can't help but gasp every time.

With no beloved city to drown the sky with light,
and no beloved Ocean to pull in clouds,
the desert brings on my head a blanket of a million city lights.

The cold now gone, I start to look, and count. Look!

There's Los Angeles! Right there. And San Diego!
Up there is San Francisco, see the Golden Gate? And Sacramento right
next.

To my right, many stars litter the night.
Ah, this must be New York!
And you have Boston up a little.
Surely that is Philadelphia! With Baltimore right next!

And so I lay,
my mind swarming with pushing put the city lights.
Seeing the uncovered stars,
and I lose a sense of size, it is truly awesome.

It is inspiring. Total. Awe."

# 30 IN MY ARMS

"From the first time you were placed
in my arms,
my heart stopped almost for too long,
just like how long I waited to meet you.

Some may question,
why you're in my arms,
and whether you should be,

but the way you look at me,
with eyes so piercing,
wandering around,
locking onto me,

I don't question my heart.
It leads me true,
and it loves your mother,
and it loves you.

Fate doesn't decide love,
and neither does blood,
for what's in a name, except nothing
but a method for identification?

No, there's so much more to it,
and loving someone is decided by the heart,
influenced sometimes by that individual or sometimes by our own morals.

This I will teach you.

But enough of that,
what matters is you,
and it's surreal how you fit in my arms.

Others will hold you,
and more will sing praise,
but to you, I sing my love,
and in my arms, you sleep,

with the love of my life
at my side,
where my love for you yourself was born,
lying next to one another,

my intent to never grow fond.
But that was futile,
for I have nothing but love for you,
who is asleep in my arms.

And we lay, and awaken,
and tend to you, her and I,
and when we lay you down,
she falls asleep,

in my arms.

I have never felt this way,
and it's because of you,
and I look forward to when I can hold you again,
in my arms."

# 31 YOURS UPON MINE

"The first time it happened,
remembered through the haze,
we were goaded into it,
you and I,

on the streets of downtown,
people bustling by to the next bar,
while we were in line,
your hand in mine.

I remember the skirt, and the blouse,
so carefully picked, and those red high heels,
though not a bright ruby, but deep,
and the way you smelled.

But what I mostly remember
is how you took me by the neck,
and we first locked lips,
both of us intoxicated, me more so,

and how intoxicating those lips were.
Which, common sense dictates,
would be blamed on the alcohol.

I now know this is preposterous!

For your lips! So full,
adorned on your face,
drive my mind in a frenzy,
when locked with mine.

Your kisses, variable upon your mood,
drive me wild with your passion,
or melted with your slow embrace,
as you enjoy the moment,
and you teach me the same.

Oh! To have you in my arms,
your body pressed against mine,
our skin; warm, touching.
Our lips; soft, dancing.

My heart beats faster,
my mouth goes dry,
my body begins to hunger,
as you lay yours upon mine.

From the littlest peck,
to the slow embrace,
from the heated action we share,
to the goodbye kiss...

yours are divine."

## 32 THE SILENT HOUND

"The canine prowls,
fiercely, for upon his back,
laid across, weighing him down,
his hard won prey will bring others to take.

But this dog, alone and unafraid
like people of lands past,
is aware his strength is cut short,
denominated by his lack of kin.

He is strong, but only one,
and he knows he cannot stand
against many, though he will,
if he must.

This dog, proud, is silent,
like an immovable oak,
his breath mighty, his hide,
coarse, like bark.

He makes his way, not slowly,
not quickly, but surely,
moving with a purpose,
and on this night,

the Moon softly throwing Her gaze
upon the meadow below,
washing it in a white glow,
glinting on the fresh snow,

the Hound stops. Silent.

He listens, intense is his stare,
into the distance he squints,
and hopes others aren't coming,
for he dreads the fight ahead.

But indeed, there they are,
another wolf pack begin to howl,
and they bust into the clearing from the edge of the woods ahead,

circling the beast and his meal,
which he sets down.

The Hound looks across,
the growling members of the pack surrounding him,
his breathe steaming into little clouds,
up past his large maw.

The wolves speak first,
and one snarls as it jumps,
but the mighty Hound bashes into him,
and brings the wolf down.

The Hound springs up,
and not a moment too late,
for he was expecting another attack,
and it was upon him before he was tall.

The Hound falls, but this mighty beast fights,
and the wolves jump in,
to finish up the night.

And then, the big Hound,
having snapped necks and tore throats,
rises to chase the three wolves left,
as they whine and dash, blood on their coats.

The Hound lost his meal,
but will not succumb to eating his kin,
and now again goes on to hunt,
and keep from starvation,

completely silent."

# 33 WHEN I WAKE

"The first thing, mostly,
that I see when I open my eyes,
is your snoozing little face.

I search for it, through the clouds of the pillows and the sea of the sheets,
and when I find that sweet face of yours,
wow! Look at you,
sound asleep.

It makes me think,
this must be what it is like,
to look upon Heaven's scenes,
and see an Angel slumber.

But then sometimes, it is you,
who trains her first sight unto me,
as you watch my chest heave,
like a machine working the furnace, its large engine pumping,
its mind quiet, for now.

And you smile, softly,
with adoration and admiration,
propping yourself on one arm,
and placing your free hand upon my face.

But the absolute best way,
moments so sweet, but not too common,
is when we arise together,
and through hazy eyes we find one another,

that first smile we share,
when I wake, that instant,
our brains still turning on,
drunk from our slumber,

is absolute magic. Oh, your smile!
Your eyes, are like a destination I can lose myself,
like a lone wanderer in a forest full of trees,
that turned into the beautiful sunset colors of fall.

And when we look upon one another,
and smile and laugh,
I give praise to the most high,
you're the one in my life.

There is no better way,
to rise. Ho! To do so
with music, well,
that's a close second.

But you.
You're the sunshine in my life.
The beat that makes me clap,
the wave that washes me anew,
the push I use to move forward,
the motivation to be a better man.

The one for me!

No better way, to see the one who makes you feel this way,

to wake. To see that person,
when you wake."

# 34 THE THEIF

"Can it be? You,
the thief!

I have heard of you,
and I know your technique!

You are the stealer of souls
the breaker of minds,
the melter of hearts.

The thief's theme,
the theme of this rhyme making me fall asleep,
I lay in debate while I wait
for your weight to press the floor
and announce your quiet entrance.

I can sense you, thief!
In the silence of tonight,
moving through the shadows,
with not your body,

or with your mind.

But with your words.

You! How dare you,
breaking into my mind like a
skilled sapper,
mining your image into my head.

I absolutely am floored by you,
you really bring me there,
I say to you now, thief,
get out of my head!

You paint my canvas with an impossibly large brush,
and encompass my soul for the moment,
as I read, with fervor,
your latest entry.

Why, thief! Why must you steal me away from my reality,
and take me for a ride,
along the many adventures you have painted just for me,
or at least I like think that, half the time.

Thief! Make your presence known,
and steal my heart again,
take my mind in the middle of the night,
take me away from this world,
spin me a tale, nothing foul!

To the farthest deserts, take me,
the blistering Sun punishing the sand below,
the wanderer doomed to his own fate,
scorpions scampering among my boots,

take me, thief!

To the deepest jungles,
positively teeming with life and sounds,
the humid air full of so many smells,
sweet from the flowers,
pungent from the standing water,
Earthy from the dirt beneath my toes,

take me, thief!

From the snowy plains of the mountains feet,
to the grand Ocean, mighty in her prowl along the coast.

From the most astonishing Empire, it's buildings sprawling with gold,
to the most humble garden, tended by the old man while his wife sits,
reading.

Thief, you steal me away.

Now? I demand it!"

## 35 ANYTHING

"I would defy the laws of nature,
pushing my fire into the Sea,
and burn as bright as ever,
for you.

I would dip into the Ocean,
face its full fury,
and dive to the bottom of the depths,
for you.

I would pass through the forest,
delve deep into the heart of darkness,
and retrieve the most forbidden fruit,
for you.

I would walk,
and fly,
and crawl,
through the Dark Corners of the Earth,
for you.

I would face the wildest beasts,
with fear in my throat,
and bravery in my heart,
for you.

I would shape the hot metal,
with a thousand hammer blows,
and pound a thousand more,
for you.

For you,
I would sing my heart out,
I would pass through fire,
sink into water,
move the Earth herself,
and bend the hands of Time.

You are my everything,
you mean the world to me.

I would go onto bended knee,
and offer you my heart for life.
Promise you the world,
and much more.

This is no attempt to satisfy,
for I have no need.
I am simply telling you the truth,
of my every will and dream.

You are my dream,
that I wander through the day with,
but with a smile adorned,
and my heart leading me true.

I love you,
and I would do anything.
You are my everything,
let me prove it."

# 36 HER SLUMBER

"She is such a bright light,
active through the day;
the middle of the night
her favorite time.

During the night,
she is as live as if it's noon,
and she don't mind whether you
can hang, she's awake!

Yes, she is quite the ride,
though she is just as readily willing,
to let you embrace her and feel her skin against hers,
and press against her and break out in that smile,

at night? Wow. She will take your breath away, for sure.
She is still warm from the day before,
and even if you can't see,
she knows exactly what to do with you.

She don't need a light,
to twist you up, this I know
to be true. Quite frankly,
she's best at night!

But my favorite time, to join our bodies,
and to feel either her kiss or squeeze?
The only time she rarely is so awake. It's a battle!

In the morning, she is cold!
Cold, indeed, and so hard to awaken.

As I slowly dip my body into hers,
generally to her empty face,
I shudder as she lightly moans in complaint,
as my skin starts to shiver.

In the morning, she is so unforgiving,
and takes a while to awaken,
with much coaxing, indeed.

Gifts? Not necessary, just patience.

I love her. In the mornings, it is so cold.
I am barely kept warm by my suit.
But I smile! It's a brand new day,
it's a brand new start,
just look at her! God, she is so beautiful,
especially at dawn.

From the mountains,
to the trees,
from the hillsides,
this is where I want to be.

Come! Breathe, and take it in.
It's so easy to love her.
This is why I face the cold fury of the morning waters.
To surf her waves, while she's cold, and empty,
is to be dedicated to the feelings she gives me, while I am blessed,
and happy, as every wave I catch in the morning makes me warmer,

warmer in my skin,
warmer in my blood,
warmer in my heart!
I cannot express

those mornings. To awaken this deep beauty,
to coax out this ride, I can't help,
but look in my heart,
and find home.

Even if the clouds cover my sky,
and it cries down on me, I smile,
for they're always be sunshine
after the rain.

With love in my heart
and that ride in my mind,
they can never keep us apart,
night or day, dusk or dawn,
never.
I love the Ocean."

## 37 THE NEXT CHAPTER, OR, BOY MEETS WORLD

"No, I don't belong,
but I sure feel at home.
I left my loves behind,
their touch still on my lips,

their memories on my mind.

But one things for certain,
maybe two things for sure,
this new land is enticing,
maybe in its backyard grows a cure.

I am weary,
my travels have been laborious,
with the worry of hauling my life with me,
tugging at my nerves like the wind tugs at my surfboards.

But I have made it,
I can rest,
fill up my reserves,
and breathe it in, this land.

Oh, what joy it is!
To be starting anew.
Not without memories,
not without lessons learned,
but with a uncommon perspective,
in this beautiful land.

Others have been here before,
And they lend me their words,
I lend them my ear.
I am excited to walk about.

But what of those whom my thoughts for reside?
Shall I tear up over the distance?
Leave what I left behind?

Nay! Why, all this does is strengthen my tie,
embeds my heart in stone,
and set the tone for my love,
for them,
for life.

They still sleep deep,
my two beauties,
she still breathes,
the other, waves still crash.

I love them,
and they push me to my new land,
and so I look ahead.

My future,
seemingly a big wide open space, has plenty of time,
and no place,
for the worries that try to flood my mind.

I will miss them,
but that's ok.
Every day that passes,
brings me closer to seeing them again!

We will be ok,
I will be just fine,
With a smile that beams,
I begin the next chapter in my life!"

*I drove across the country from California to Tennessee, on account of orders from the Marine Corps.*

*Let's start with what I left.*
*First, I left a wonderful woman, who decided to stick with me during the move. I also left behind the Pacific Ocean, and if you've read this far you know I'm a very avid surfer.*

*This move was very big; I had never been in the South before. Read on and watch how my writing, and my life, grew and developed.*

# 38 THE FESTIVAL

"The festival is today!
And today, I had been happy for,
for I was to be present,
and all who shall see these present,
greetings.

This will be a grand day!
Many will be merry,
and many will partake in drink!
Oh, to be a part of these festivities
is common and expected!

I would have been there,
and made quite the feast,
or at least,
a piece of the cornucopia!

But,
as unlikely as we want to believe,
and admit,
this festival is not enjoyed by all...

there are other pressing matters,
and though today we have made a point,
a point to push those matters away,
Life will not be ignored,
and it will march on as it always has.

Indeed, today,
the day of the festival,
there are those who will not watch the tournament,
and instead will be watching us.

We, few warriors,
having earned our place in these lands,
are asked to lay one of our own to rest.

We, warriors all,
have been called upon to give respects to our fellow brother,
who gave the ultimate sacrifice,
so that others didn't have to.

At first, dismay! No,
but the festival! The tournament!
I don't want to miss the match!
The joy of being a part of it,
as it only happens once a year!
How frustrating!

And then,
how immediately ashamed I am,
to have let myself feel this way.

Today is not the festival.
Today, for a family,
is the day their loved one is laid down,
is given his passing into reality,
and is sadly going somewhere
that the only thing he can take
is his name.

That is my duty. That is
where I will be.

And so today,
instead of filling the viewing box,
and enjoying the morning crowds,
I instead polish my shoes.

Instead of joining the afternoon den,
and raising my voice with the crowd,
I join those who mourn.

I salute,
and pay my respects,
to the one who isn't here,
to enjoy the festival.

And that is what is important.
Today isn't a festival.
Today is the day,
a warrior's family receives
a folded flag.

This is my place,
and I will be there,
proudly.

The festival is forgotten."

# 39 EVERY DAY

"Today, to most, is a day,
where we celebrate the love,
or lack thereof,
that we share with our love.

To love,
and be loved,
is to be alive, to
perhaps,
have a greater purpose.

True love,
the kind that exists between the
truest of lovers,
makes us flutter,
fly, strive
to be better.

A love
that makes you feel better,
be better,
is truly something to celebrate.

The love we share,
my love,
is of the rarest kind,
the finest quality,

like the brightest diamond,
the softest silk,
the aged, crisp wine,
the most decadent tart.

But as I walk,
along the side of no one
but everyone else's love,
I can't help but wonder:

what is so special about today?
I do not see the point
of the plastic flowers,

the cheap chocolates,
just another way those,
who maybe do not know love,
fulfill their love of money instead.

Not all intentions are bad,
for love is always pure,
but to you, my love,
I have a proposal.

Not the most original,
but why not, every day,
celebrate the love we have?

Every day, I am thankful you are
in my life.
Every day, I celebrate your heart and soul,
and how we coincide.

You're my everything,
and today,
the way I feel,
is how I feel about you,

Every day.

So today, I will call you mine,
and hope you call me yours, too,
but I sleep tonight knowing,
that I can call you mine,
Every day."

# 40 TRIALS

"And here I sit,
alone in this coffee shop,
crowded from my left and my right,
couples deciphering their own little lives.

How insignificant,
their trials seem to me,
but only a second before I realize
how smaller still my own seem.

The couple on my left,
two girls inseparable,
whisper their own misgivings of their misunderstood love.
They mill about,
nervous to display their touching hands and sneaked kisses.

The couple on my right,
deep in their own little world,
discuss their own existence in the world I claim,
and they're inches away from each other,
speaking in hushed voices,
but I hear every word.

And here I sit,
my own little trial about to begin,
with a removed situation in an aforementioned circumstance,
so heavy,
keeping me happy, but my mind busy,
and I am beginning to spin,
not sure if I am losing focus on one or the other.

My new trials are insanely simple,
and appear to be incredibly easy,
but I know if I don't pay heed I'll slip,
and lose traction on this fast moving floor with
its own obstacle course.

The distance that keeps us apart,
the same that spin my head away from my heart,
the same that keep my skin away from the salt
of the Earths own vibe,

would be crushing to lesser men.
But who am I to assume that I,
a simple man who shouldn't bloviate,
am cut of finer cloth?

I feel the pressure push my head,
like as though the world is coming down,
but I spin my perception upside down,
and see that it is I, myself,

who have put myself onto my own head!
And that it is the Earth doing as she always has,
and pulls me down to Her.

There is no weight on my shoulders!
I am standing on my head,
and I laugh at the selfishness that has brought me
to perceive my own problems and issues
to have been brought on by the world.

Instead,
stand up, you fool!
I am clouding my head with unnecessary things,
what I should focus on are the things
that truly matter.

My trial over,
I turn to her,
and call her,
and confess to her
the love that I have
not been relaying.

She is my everything,
and so I let her know,
with the fear of rejection,
no matter how probable,
finally washed away.

I finally stand back up,
and breathe deep,
and begin to think back to the beginning
of this night.

At this coffee shop.

Where I sat here not to
write about anyone else.

Just my own,
foolish trial.
Self-inflicted,
and self-professed.

And now, self-conquered."

# 41 SNOWFALL

"My heart belongs to one,
and only one,
but she gladly accepts my love for another.

Every day,
my skin itches,
and the only way I can feed my hunger,
for that beloved rush,
is the thrill of the ride,
the chase of the tide,
the hunter of the swell.

I am a wave warrior,
I am an armed veteran,
my weapon, a blade,
a buster of clouds.

But the clouds I cut,
are the dreams of those who fly,
the softest glides,
with the help of the monstrous might of Her deep breath!

The good Mother Earth,
ah, the Lady who evokes me,
pushes her Vibe unto me,
manifesting my ride to the shore.

I glide,
the sound of the wave breaking behind me,
the song of my Lady Ocean,
the song she sings to me.

The song of her waves,
breaking on the sand,
soothes my soul,
like a song I lay a child to sleep to,
only bested by the way I feel
when I hold my one true love.

My Love!
Oh, the poetry she evokes me to write,
stands toe to toe to the words my Ocean inspires me to spin together.

And some must imagine,
Why, this poet and his lover
must spend hours in the water,
surfing the waves of life and love together,
out on the Ocean!

Nay! My Love does not share my love
for the Ocean blue.

She enjoys the waves crashing,
and following the sun as it sinks in the horizon,
but she turns away the idea
of being out on the lineup.

Is this a concern?
No! For I, myself,
share the same level of uneasiness of her own element.

Like the beautiful,
sweet,
sparkle of her smile,
the fresh white snow that now adorns my ground,
brings the glint of snow from her smile out to be enjoyed by the world.

Now her smile, it has always melted me,
but the snowstorm that brings so many joy?

In it, I frown! Something
I rarely ever do.
The snow, I do not enjoy,
it brings a groan out from my mouth,
as I trudge through its new trials it throws onto me.

The snow!
It should go,
it should melt,
I cannot stand its cold.

I want to be in the Ocean,
the vibe pulsing onto my skin.

The snow is not of the Mother Earth's own vibe. Right?

Now, I stop.

And think back to the roots of my own soul search,
and the ride I yearn to find...

is also hunted on this disliked medium!
What kind of conditions,
could cause this to become true,
and the actions to be taken for such a ride.

Why, my Love,
she has no weapon or blade,
but she has a touch of love,
as she glides in the snow.

Where I feel powerless,
she finds grace.
Where she feels the same,
I am at home.

She finds peace,
where I may panic.
Where my Love is uneasy,
I am in touch with my soul.

Where I am of skin,
unconstrained from my water armor,
she is wrapped up snug,
and happy to be so warm.

So ironic,
Her unspoken love for her medium,
never was crystal clear,
until I find myself inches in it.

Ironic, still,
was her fear of my Ocean,
I never realized how much it rang true.

Yet she is willing, still,
to paddle out with me,
and I truly know now,
it is not out of a new found love for the salty sea,
but her unconditional love for me.

And so,
I walk outside,
not because I have fallen in love with the sparkly white fluff...

But because in a way...

I am closer to the one
who wishes nothing more
than be in her element
with me."

# 42 TWO WAYS OF LIFE

"To be interested,
in one way or another,
in the way we lead our lives,
and how it may differ from one another,
is to establish a hunger for more fulfilling life.

My own life,
well, to begin that tale,
is one of many facets and considerations,
but to be quaint,

the culmination of all the events
that has lead me to where I am,
is its own wild entity.

And so we all are!
Isn't it beautiful? To think
that we all, at one point,
begin to shape how we lead our lives,

and it still grows every second,
or at least is should,
since weakness grows from idleness.

Now, to begin this examination,
even in that it may or may not be warranted,
it would be wise to start with how I approach
the day, and its impact on my growth.

I am balanced,
as I glide down the face of the wave,
my board my own lonely plane,
its wax my roots,

my feet digging in and out,
rocking back and forth,
pushing my own journey down the Earths own vibe.

I am blessed,
as I walk to and fro from the streets shops
to the bed I share with such a beauty.

My hands, my blessed skill of use,
instruments of creation,
of healing, of constructing,
of bending metal into monstrous machines,
and dancing words across the paper for my newest painting.

I am joyous,
always taking things for what they are meant to be,
the beautiful light they all have imbued within.

In each person,
each event,
and even in the darkest corners of the Earth,
I always find the bright side of life.

Now, is this way of life
limited to one who has found the joy of he'enalu?

Or can it be shared with the ultimate goal of Moksha?

The liberation of mind, body, and soul
has been sought out by myself,
and through my life I have discovered a method
I thought to be unique.

And though I am unique,
I am not unique in that I am the only one
who is different,

and the journey
for the unity
of my soul and being
has been shared for hundreds of years.

Hundreds!

The art of wave catching,
something as familiar to me as a poem,
or pen,
as I have grown to know the Ocean and its
mystifying beauty,

is a way of life.
But there are others!

Stricken from his beloved Ocean
this soul surfer has found a new wave to ride.

His new board is his mat,
his new wave, his own body,
riding each push of the Earth vibes,
through his own roots!

The roots he makes,
planting his feet,
mixing the spirit of his gross body,
and his Vital breath,
with the journey,
the goal,

of the unity of a Waves spirit.
To borrow, if you will,
that energy, and transmit,
through my body and board,
into Art.

That soulful use
of all my Chakras
to truly ascend a liberation,
I now do so without the surf,

but with the teachings of those who so long ago,
rooted themselves and delved deep
into their own minds, bodies, and souls,

and reached that peace.

The way of life I have embraced,
now intertwined with another,
he'enalu, and calling myself a soul surfer
are imbued with my newfound title of yogi.

My journey continues,
the lesson of one,
transmit to the other,
and I look ahead with positivity,

for I will reach that goal.
That Moksha.

With these two ways of life."

# 43 DIABOLICAL

"How twisted,
and let that word sink in
before I go on;

how twisted,
is the cursed warrior,
that demon,
who took all from those we loved so much!

How heartless,
is the swiftness he strikes others down,
and without a second glance,
without batting an eye,

ending a man's life like it is nothing,
as though he carelessly swats a fly.

How corrupt,
this ronin, this rogue,
his blade dancing around the air,
and slipping through our hearts and souls.

He cuts us down,
he ends our career,
and this demon makes our lives
come to an end.

He is ruthless,
unfair,
a cycle constantly running,

his only attempt to absolve of sin
is attempting to seek divine guidance,
but the very demon of revenge, himself,
runs deep in us all,
and it murders us all.

The want for revenge,
that hated love,
is so sweet when it first crosses our mind,
and that's when the demon has already cut us down.

It may be as soft as a slow kiss,
from a beautiful stranger you pass by
or a sweet embrace,
from a long, lost love.

But no matter who we are,
and no matter what we imagine it to be,
the real, twisted purpose of that momentary reprieve
is nothing more than a ruse.

The murderer has entered our hearts,
we have let him in.

Now, anger ensues,
as the demon unleashes his first weapon upon us,
and our heads fill with a rage,
that we lost control of our morality.

Even those who have attained a higher capacity
for the rough and upsetting world
can fall victim to this state,
and that's when the demon,
unsheathing his blade,

brings it to bear
above our heads.

And then we strike.

We hurt others,
we do things we normally wouldn't,
we plan, and suffer the whole time,
and lie to ourselves when we have done our deed,

lying that we have finished what they have started,
that we are at peace,
but that is the lie of the demon,
and what have we done?

We have done the opposite,

hurting the other. Breaking hearts,
breaking faces. Piercing lungs,
piercing souls.

Ruining the lives of the loved ones
of the one who hurt ours,

and the Demon laughs heartily,
his blade already ran through,
before we realize what we have done.

Do not seek revenge.

People will hurt us,
things will hurt the ones we love.

But justice is not served
when we take it in our own hands.

Others will disagree,
but those would hurt
without a moment's hesitation.

They don't have love in their hearts,
the demon having already conquered them.

Win this fight,
slay this demon,
and learn to let go.

For nothing is as diabolical
as a person with nothing to lose
and cause to fight for.
Die for.
Or worse. Kill for.

These are the wrong reasons.
Don't forget this.

Lest the demon slay you!"

# 44 THE DANCE

"I walk in,
and though my body is warm,
my muscles, unbound,
I do not know if I want to be here.

I love to move my body,
to push and pull the Earth,
and I let the Earth move me,
with her own sweet vibe.

Along with my newest joy,
one of a connection of mind,
soul, and the body I am learning
to pose into sublimity.

So here, I enter,
this hot room,
having just practiced the aforementioned art,

and the lights,
or lack thereof,
casts shadows across the walls,
as too few lanterns, alit,
dance their flame's light
all over the dark mats.

We few,
awkwardly spaced out around the edge,
sway slowly as the music begins,
slow tunes that creep into my skin,
and fill me up with movement.

I close my eyes, and try to lose
all senses,
as I sway back and forth,
dancing with the music
as well as breathe.

I open my eyes,
and move around the floor,
glancing across the room,
to watch others, like me,
dance to their own souls.

One dancer, a young yogi,
flutters around the deck,
arms swimming through the air,
like a ballerina.

Another, an older artist,
sweeps her feet around her body,
her hands flow in and out,
like a pulsing, bright star.

My own dance,
changes with the song.

One of them, I am the Ocean,
my legs planted, like roots,
and my arms are waves,
crashing into the shore!

I sway, low and then high!
And bring my hands,
the crest of the wave,
fiercely into the ground!

Another, I am a warrior,
the best of my tribe,
spinning and jumping to the war drums,
hyping the hunting party,
for the villages next trip!

I glance again,
time nonexistent,
music moving in and out,
the bass hitting me as we all change our dance.

Now, we are at a night club,
dancing to the electronic beat,
respecting the space of one another,
but enveloping the whole room
with our energy.

One Dancer,
a tall man,
swings is head and torso around,
like a giant bell,
tolling its ring,
into the towers square.

Another, my friend,
is plainly smiling as he dances
with no expertise,
moving around the floor in every way
that is fun and comical.

The songs blur together,
we few, Dancers all,
meld our minds, bodies, and souls,
and let it all out.

Now, the music slows,
as does our movement,
the room filled with our heat,
and alit with nothing but dancing silhouettes.

We slow to a crawl,
now many on the floor,
melting into poses,
counter poses,
inversions,
and meditation.

We all end together,
one inhale,
one exhale,
one breath,

some of us lending our voice,
with the music that permeates the walls,
connecting us all,
and I was sure to give my Om.

We finish,
my senses returning to me,
my muscles become aware
of how tired I now am.

What a dance.

And now, I just want a feast!"

# 45 MY MOTHER

"My Mother
is my hero.

She taught me,
raised me,
by herself, no less,
and while doing so,
imbued within me,

the lessons she had learned herself.

From the sunrays that broke through my blinds
in the morning when I was a child,
to the day I left the rainy Pacific Northwest,
to learn about myself in ways of old,

she has always been there.

I am a US Marine,
like my father before me,
and his father before him.

But I did not join because of them.
To be frank,
I don't know them.

But my Mother,
the toughest woman in my life,
got me started on a pathway
that would transfer into an ever-growing journey.

My Mother
taught me how to love.
She taught me to give my heart,
unconditionally,
and to be vulnerable.

She taught me how to treat a woman.
The difference between loving our other half,
and 'claiming' your 'right'
to the most beautiful thing in a man's life.

My Mother
taught me to be strong.
To give everything into what I do,
and to never falter.
To rise, to fight, to believe
in myself.

She gave her Son
everything she had.
She gave her boy,
her own flesh and blood,
the life she wish she had.

Maybe we didn't have everything,
and even that was a class,
my healthy contempt for comfort
has made my life no chore.

My Mother
is my hero
because she made me the man
I am today.

I do not even come close,
to expressing my debt to her,
the long nights she stayed up,
tears on both of our faces,
wishing life was different.

But the day she watched me march
across the parade deck,
where so many Marines before me have done.

And she watched me march
from the review box with generals,
her Son the top graduate,
she beamed with affection.

Every moment in time blurred,
every time I pushed her back,
every time I ran into her arms,
and every time I made her proud,

poured out into one moment of completion.

"That's my son," she said,
and it was because of her,
that I have grown
into the selfless person I strive to be.

To give,
to sacrifice,
she gave me the gift
to enjoy doing so.

To serve is its own reward.
To never give in.
To love.

This is why
my Mother
is my hero."

# 46 THE CUT

"The shop is full,
many patrons sitting in line,
and in this land,
the wait is long.

They all sit in front
of where they will hopefully be next,
to sit in the chair
for a trim of their hair.

And the little Boy,
sitting on the booster,
looks across with anxiety,
as the clipper nears his ear.

The buzzing, like a fly,
purrs menacingly,
making the youth cringe,
and drawing a groan from the barber.

He looks around,
ignoring his Father, asking for his discipline,
ignoring his Mother, trying to sooth his nerves,
and locks eyes with a man across the room.

Not a man. A statue!

This man, built like a machine.
The boy looks in wonder at this stoic.
His muscles tightly wrapped,
his chest broad, filling the chair he sits in,
his shoulders brushing the patrons to his left and right.

He sits, relaxed, but still up straight,
his gaze burns through his glasses not with intensity,
but a low glow,
like the last warm ember after a raging fire.

He looks at the Boy,
and his face turns into a smile,
contradictory to his stature,
and the little one smiles back.

The Boy's two parents look at the Man,
as he softens his statue,
going from stone to flesh
as the Man leans onto his knees with his elbows.

The little Boy looks at the Man,
and stops.
Wait! His hair is so short!

"You don't need a haircut!"
the Boy tells the Man.
"Your hair is so short,
don't get it cut again!"

And then the Man laughs,
a deep, booming burst,
that fills the room with joy
that surprises the shop.

The Mother, having sat,
leans and asks the Man,
"What do you do for a living?
How you make your pay?"

And the man, with a smile,
replies with a little bit of thunder:
"Ma'am, I'm a U.S. Marine,
I shoot artillery."

The Boy beams,
the Father looks approvingly,
the Mother begins to interview the Man,
and the shop nods with smiles.

The Boy asks,
"Why do you need a haircut?"
and the Man answers,
"Because I'm supposed to look sharp!"

Well, the Boy thinks,
I want to look sharp, too!
And before he could ask his dad,
the barber exclaims, "All done!"

"Wait, what?
I'm already all done?
But I didn't even feel it!"
and the audience laughs.

The family pays, and the boy walks by,
and as they push through the door,
he looms back to his seat he had sat,
and sees the Marine,
looking dead ahead,
his face returned to stone.

But his smirk remained."

## 47 THE CIGARETTE

"The storyteller passes her,
and stops short off his ride,
glancing over to his excuse,
to stop his push along in life.

Sister leaned against the wall,
cigarette between her fingertips,
inhaling her cloud in through her lips,
she has that gift,

that gravity to pull at my wit
to find a way into a conversation
which I wish she'd partake,
and so I try, and ask her name.

She says her name,
and I take her hand in mine
and shake the greeting slowly by,

and in no time,
the moment passed,
as I blurred away,
almost falling over
into the rack of bikes down the walk.

And then I stop,
thinking back to the days
where I'd lay there burning
through a pack of 20 squares

thinking about where my life would be at 20,
and 22, and afterwards the age that melts together,

as I blindly push down the street,
running into my neighbor's board, and into a pole.

Lost in thought at the meeting,
intention innocent as always,
just a brother hailing a sister,
due to the guidance of his mother.

And then I stop,

gathering my thoughts,
skating past the local coffee shop,
floating down the street
like the wind, breathing in,
like...

That lonely square I'd take,
leaning against the concrete,
blowing clouds into the air
completely unaware
of the future meeting I'd share
with the sister and her soft stare,

that would make me think
back and forth through time,
in a system not so jaded,
and reflect on this life of mine,

and smile at the end,
the night coming to a close,
putting up my board,
and laying said head on the bed,
satisfied with where I am today,

and maybe if I'm lucky,
can move forward to say,

I've only gotten better."

# 48 THE SPIRIT OF THE BOARDS

"I am like a mountain,
legs spread wide,
rooted, like great roots,
feet flat against the board.

We are one, this board,
this inanimate object,
and I breathe life into it,
as we glide along Life.

The board has my soul,
it is a piece of me.
It is more than a piece of fiberglass
more than epoxy.

It is my Buster, my Blade,
my weapon of the Waves,
and with it I dance, or try,
and share the energy of the Ocean for a moment.

The Ocean, my beloved Lady,
pulses her vibe into my veins,
and the conveyor, what I sit upon,
is this board.

At one time it was just a board,
at one time it was just a purchase,
but now having shared my life on it,
poured my soul into it,
it has its own spirit.

Out in the water,
I splay my palm upon the wax,
the water droplets running down the jagged maze it makes,
back into the Ocean herself.

My love for surfing
is a single water droplet
in the sea spray of emotion
that courses this world.

It almost doesn't matter.

Yet! That love is a part of me,
and evoked out from me,
out of my whole heart.

My soul is in that board.

But alas! The Ocean has left me,
rather, I left her,
and my spirit no longer can ride!

What is a man to do
when he has no way to search out his soul?
When he has no way to find himself,
find his center, his reason to be alive?

He continues to do what he loves,
he finds a way, and in that way,
he learns that there are more than one way
to find that Zen.

I still surf,
but along the streets,
along the concrete and bricks,
not perplexed with little tricks,

atop of this board,
floating along wheels,
it carrying me over the walk on the road,
up and down the waves of the hills.

My board garners me looks,
and unintentional judgment,
but the life of a surfer isn't defined
by what others think of him.

My board, having shrunk,
from seven feet to forty inches,
wax to grip tape,
fins to wheels,

has my soul, indeed,
and rides along its own course,
it has its own spirit.

The spirit is of a warrior,
one who wanders,
but is not lost.

It is strong, it is deep,
and it is thinking,
searching,
and surfing for that final place,

where I find my heart pure,
my mind clear,
and my soul,

clean."

# 49 AFTER PRACTICE

"My body is warm,
having been in the hearth,
and though the blade is in the water,
the heat still sizzles deep inside.

The winding-down begins,
my appetite becomes biting,
my thirst, drowning my focus,
my body wet to touch.

I come down,
my mat rolled up,
my clothes replaced,
my water being drunk.

Along with these things, my focus returns,
and not from a scattered state,
but from the state that I seek out every practice,
that sole focus on my breath.

Instead of that mindset,
where my mind and body melds together,
it becomes multi-faceted,
and sprawls all around to everything all at once.

My mind begins its dance,
jumping from one subject to the next,
bowing to each part of my day ahead,
leaving behind the practice that was so restorative.

Coffee in hand,
biscuit already gone,
my body's needs are satisfied,
my mind returns to the task at hand.

Reaching for the sun,
letting it lay onto my skin,
I press the street beneath my feet,
feeling the vibe of the city on this Sunday morning.

I begin to float,
the practice unknowingly setting the pace for the day,
my mind moving to my one true love,
waiting for me, patiently, in the land of Gold,

in which I will fly to her.
But not today,
and instead I breathe in this land of Volunteers,
of those who so long ago rose up,

like I rose up this morning
to bend into shape my body.
Bend into shape my mind.
Bend into shape my soul.

So much energy,
expended at practice,
but I am not running on reserves,
instead full of life.

Recent days past,
the sky tears fell heavy,
and it made our walks slow,
turning the Earth to mud.

But with that comes beauty,
for no Lotus grows without mud,
and so we all rise,
and rejoice instead of refrain the past clouds.

I transition,
from my mind that so often wanders off
to the settings around me,
and enjoy the day that is.

Feeling great,
this glorious day upon us,
let us meditate through the chalice,
the sweet plant, good life
with the breath I savor

that I am allowed after practice."

# 50 THEY ARE ASLEEP

"I cannot believe it.
I am here.
Next to her,
the one I dream about.

The missing piece to my puzzle.
Sailing on uncharted seas,
that her and I call our love,
I am not haunted by insecurities.

24 hours can feel longer than what's right,
looking back at where I was the other night,
and the previous one I have woken up from,
there are differences, of space and time.

Here, I sit,
my heart overflowing with emotion,
as it always is,
but this time it is uncontrollable.

I could take a picture,
of the smile that is on my face,
the background switched to that old scene,
a clear blue sky littered with palm trees.

But what that photograph won't show,
is who I'll wake up with tomorrow,
and the identity of that love
is the reason I even came.

To put my feelings into words
almost seems difficult,
when I frown in the fact
that I pour out fantasies in minutes!

But in this quiet instant,
the first since I came home to her,
I write with love in my heart
and a beautiful scene right before me.

On that bed,
where many times I have laid my body to rest,
let my heartbeat, which is always running high,
finally slow down,
let my mind unwind,

she lays.

She is asleep,
though not out of boredom or distaste,
but out of desire,
her heart succumbed to the joy
that I am here again.

Her eyes closed,
her head rests on a pillow
which splays her hair all over
to give her the crown she deserves.

Covered by a soft, white blanket
to keep her warm,
curled up as though she is adorned
in an angelic white dress.

Her breath is easy,
her perfect sweet lips are in a slight smile,
I leave her be
to return to the one who sits beside me now.

This one,
this sweet child,
softly snores his nap away,
his belly full,
his needs attended.

This one,
staring at me as soon as I have walked in,
makes me think he remembers
all the times I sang to him in my arms.

All the times I stood up,
and swept him up as he cried,
and soothed him back to sleep,
while his Mother snoozed next to us.

They are asleep,
but I do not mind.

I let her sleep,
for I know she has lost sleep.
Though maybe not over me,
she will appreciate that I give her time.

All the time she and I spent together
sleeping in each other's caress.
I have always cherished that time,
our bodies recuperating from the day before.

Or the night just before.
 I smile at this thought,
and then return my gaze to the little one
watching his chest rise and fall.

I let him sleep,
this sweet child,
for though he will awaken soon,
his soft moments resting
help him grow.

I can't be wrong for loving them,
for I love them so much.
Perhaps too much?

Well, if that was a crime,
then I would be a criminal.
Because loving them so much,
too much,
feels so right.

My heart is bursting,
my eyes are welling up,
as I take a look out the window,
and feel the sun on my face.

And then that song comes on,
one of the first I ever sang to this child,
and I become overwhelmed with emotion,
my hand shakes as I write.

Together, we can make some memories,
and help love, grow, and live eternally,
and spread this word over both land and sea,
and help each other on this long hard journey.

Love is what life costs,
and I pay in full.
Yesterday, today,
and tomorrow.

I cannot believe,
they have slept so long,
well, maybe him,
having slept through the night
she and I shared.

But I am grateful,
just to be here again,
to have them in my arms,
to kiss their foreheads.

To share more moments,
to make them smile,
to tend to their needs,
to spend a little while.

I am so grateful,
to have come back home,
and see the woman I call mine,
and the child who has my eternal adoration.

These two,
my heart I give to them,
and only them,
and it is forever theirs to keep.

I want to shout,
so happy and in love,
but instead keep quiet,
for they are asleep."

*This poem is an attempt to capture the utter joy felt, having waited to the morning after the first night of visiting California again. Namely, the woman that called me her one and only.*

# 51 GIVING UP

"Sometimes,
it feels like the worlds on your shoulders.
Sometimes,
it feels like everything is crashing down.
Sometimes,
we can't drink fast enough from the cup.
Sometimes,
we give up.

We give up what once was glory,
what once we woke up and exclaimed
our joy for having.
But now we wonder.

The pain that draws its breath
upon my quiet sorrow
deepens the wound that I have.
And no one would stand for that.

We would give up.
We would move on.
We would go for something else.
We would dive deep into an unknown pool;

its depth unknown,
just for the relief of the cool water
on our skin,
relieving us from the pain.

I love the water.

But I love you more!

Pain can be crippling,
it can bring us to our knees,
it can pull from our throats surrender,
it can pull from our eyes tears.

But I do not let that dissuade me,
I do not let that keep me down.
I just can't stop trying,
as you won't either.

Others would have left long ago,
not because it isn't worth it,
but because their attention spans no length,
their hunt for instant satisfaction hungry.

Instead, I will wait,
for you,
and time and event will continue to test us,
as it has already.

Let them come;
I will not give up.
You're worth it,
and that won't change.

Emotions may run all over,
and words may spin out,
but love won't ever disappear;
my heart leads me true.

It leads me to be with you,
it leads me through
to be the one
you want in your life.

Because I want you, too.

My thoughts on giving up?
Never."

# 52 THE FIRST RIDE

"Wheels pulled away,
bearings stripped bare.
Nuts loosened
and screws fed out.

The board lays bare,
the wave rider naked.

No fins to turn in the water.
Or, rather,
no trucks to turn on the street.
But there is a purpose!

The dirty, silver trucks
are tossed away in a dramatic fashion,
clattering across the floor.
That old hardware

had swept me up and down
the concrete ocean.
These concrete waves
that give me relief.

These waves I yearn for.
Instead of the mist of the Ocean,
my fingers graze the leaves of the sidewalk trees.
Instead of dodging surfers,
I dodge pedestrians.

The trucks are installed, new,
orange and blue,
matching the massive wheels
that will bear me over the grey, dry cement.

The board, assembled,
is handed back,
and already I feel the heat
of the potential ride that awaits me.

I stop, and look across the lineup,
no other surfer looking to drop in my wave,
I drop my heavier board and push off,
immediately feeling the new response sway me to and fro.

I kick, and adjust my drive,
my new wheels pouring out past the edge of my foot's usual path,
and push again,
zipping down the block much faster than I am used to.

Like a wave that somehow grows to a much bigger monster
between the time you paddled out to catch it,
and you have that split second, just a split,
where you decide to paddle as hard as you can out of its way,
or turn, swallow your fear, and catch your biggest ride.

I swallow my fear,
dominate this wave,
and catch the fastest ride on this new board,
pushing effortlessly through downtown.

I learn and play with my new curves,
my ridiculous turning radius bending at my will,
wrapping around corners and light poles,
around others with looks of distaste
and keen interest.

Some in awe,
some with smiles,
watching me ride my wave.
My mind lost in the Ocean I created myself.

This first ride rushed me here,
where I now sit,
my mind spinning,
my soul, still. At peace."

# 53 THE WAKER

"The alarm goes off
in the dark, metal cell of a room,
the berthing the soldier sleeps in.
The Waker is awoken.

He jumps in a startle,
his single wool blanket slung lazily onto the deck,
hands groping for his opticals
in the glow of the pulsing red light.

The Waker jumps out of his rack,
grabbing trousers from the bulkhead
and throwing them on along with his blouse.
He fumbles boots on and pushes the port open.

"Gangway! Gangway!" the Waker screams,
running past other troops in the tight passageway,
twisting and turning along the spiraling corridors
of the mighty Warship that sails.

The Waker has no skill,
no military prowess.
He would not last on the lines of battle,
having failed the training of the Bipedals.

He would not last as a pilot,
having no dexterity for bearing
Tanks or any of the Airwing to lay waste
against enemy lines.

The great might of the War Machine he belongs to
has more weapon systems than any other faction could oppose.
Many wars have been won on the extraordinary courage
that he wish he had, had he chose.

But alas, the Waker is weak,
his body too frail for war,
but his mind is sharp,
and so, entrusted to him, a weapon of ancient power.

Pride of the fleet,
the Warship sailed the clouds, housing the 1st War Machine.
The ship must have dropped anchor above the newest campaign,
for the Waker was summoned to his post.

Wheezing, the dark passageways
in this part of the Warship
full of cold air, The Waker
pulls to stop at his destination.

A massive door, one usually bolted shut,
was asked to be opened, and it complained,
its ancient cogs whirled against one another.
It swung open to let a heavy presence seep into the air.

The Waker stepped into the corridor,
and in this sacred atrium,
a Machine slept.
Even the air around Him was holy.

A single ray of light stole down
and silhouetted the Machine,
this bipedal behemoth, this old warrior,
the ancient weapon, the Juggernaught.

This was the precious charge
the Waker was given.
When the time came,
to wake the Hero of Mankind.

The Waker begins his lamentations,
muttering to himself as he coaxes the beast awake.
And slowly, eerily,
a deep inhale and exhale is heard.

And then the Juggernaught speaks.

<GO AWAY.>

The Waker smiles
and speaks,
as if greeting his oldest,
and only, friend. The only purpose of his existence.

"My Lord. It is time, again. We need you awake."

<NO. IT IS NOT. I DO NOT WISH IT.
SO I WILL SLEEP, AGAIN.>

The Waker sighs. Always so stubborn to rise.

 Intimidating, to prepare the Juggernaught for drop,
as the military's personal angels of death.
These giant, walking monsters that break enemies,
progress campaigns and turn the  tide of a war.

One per select War Machines,
and the Waker's own Juggernaught was the mightiest,
having won an entire war by itself.
The absolute embodiment of a fighting spirit.

Each Juggernaught, a living tomb,
had one warrior encased,
but this was no pilot like the rest.
Nay, this was something deeper.

From wars past, in the thousands of years
that Humanity has fought the Xenos across the stars,
where many have fallen on foreign lands;
planets unnamed in campaigns forgotten. During these,

some soldiers were deemed to be kept from dying.
Used was technology that should have not worked,
ancient techniques lost to time,
and methods almost more alchemy than science.

These war heroes are kept alive,
to fight another day.
A millennia later,
in their own bristling sarcophagus.

Such is their fate,
for long before sins of our father's fathers
brought the wrath of the enemy upon mankind,
war was, always has been, and always will be

their destiny.

So in his short existence,
this frail Waker,
now has at his hands,
the fiercest Juggernaught.

And his task is to awaken the ancient killer.

"Marcavius, it is time. You must awaken!
You must give your hand to the fight,
you must stride into battle,
like fables told of you doing so long ago!"

<NO! I WILL NOT ABIDE.
YOU AND YOUR WARS ARE PETTY,
I DO NOT CARE TO FIGHT.
GO AND DIE.>

The Waker narrows his focus,
turning to the console to his left,
and pushes the controls
to push adrenaline to the Juggernaught.

<YOU AWAKEN ME WITH DRUGS!
I WILL KILL YOU,
DOMINIC. MOST LIKELY.>
And the Machine stands up.

 The Waker is stunned aback by,
the whoosh and whir of the Juggernaught
blowing his hair and uniform lapels about.
"My Lord, you must be slow!"

 This was not good.
"The battle wages below,
and you will descend, but we must take time!
I cannot rush you off, you'll be in pain"

And the Juggernaught bends slightly,
as if imaginary eyes peer down onto the Waker.
And then a roar booms out,
shaking the pillars of the war ship,

<DOMINIC! DO NOT PREACH TO ME ABOUT PAIN!
THEY KILLED MY ENTIRE FAMILY,
THEY CAME, TORTURED, RAPED AND PILLAGED!
I WAS SEVEN YEARS OLD, AND THE ONLY SURVIVNG
WITNESS!>

And the Waker, shivering,
falls to his knees in fear.
Immediate relief floods him as Juggernaught speaks again,
in his stony voice at a softer volume,

<I HAVE DESTROYED ENTIRE CIVILIZATIONS.
I HAVE WATCHED MY COMRADES TURNED INTO DUST.
I HAVE SEEN INTO THE DEPTHS OF THE WORST OF MAN
AND XENOS ALIKE. I SLEEP WITH THAT. FOR ETERNITY.>

The console lights up,
the monitoring system alerting the Waker
the Machine is ready for war.
It is time.

"I am sorry, Marcavius. I did not mean
to be so ignorant.
I truly am a waste, having never fought myself,
with no idea of what you speak of."

 <NO. YOU KNOW MANY THINGS.
I HAVE SHARED TALES OF HEROISM LONG FORGOTTEN,
ABOUT ENEMIES THAT DO NOT EXIST,
OF THE TRUE NATURE OF WAR.>

The Juggernaught steps to a large droppod.
In doing so, the officers on the bridge of the Warship
know to deploy the Machine,
firing from the belly of the war ship its terrible cargo.

<THE TIME IS NOW. THERE IS ONLY WAR!
ONLY PEOPLE LIKE YOU AND ME CAN STOMACH THIS.
THERE WILL BE NO VICTORY. NO END.
BUT I WILL ENDURE. I WILL FACE MY DESTINY.>

and before the Waker can respond,
a giant buzz sounds off,
and a port slams from the ceiling, closing the drop pod
from the rest of the room.

The pod sinks, and then disappears down below,
now hurtling to jump into the midst of battle.
The dim light of the atmosphere
pouring in as the outer port shuts.

Rejoice!
No enemy will know mercy,
all will be crushed,
under the might of Marcavius.

The Waker falls against the bulkhead behind him,
floored by what the Juggernaught has said.
His destiny? But what of mine?
I won't live more than a half century.

He contemplates his own life,
of rushing to and from his room,
to awaken this monster,
a master of war and death,

yet who stresses the importance of life.

Maybe not literally.
But for a moment, the interpretation
was heavy on the Waker's mind.
There is no end. But we must accept that.

The Juggernaught has,
and he faces it with his best.
His only purpose is war.
The Waker's only purpose was also war.

\*\*\*\*

Time passes, as it always does,
and the Waker is back in the atrium,
the room crowded by mechanics and medics,
tending to the war torn Juggernaught.

"Well met, Marcavius! Where have you been?
What have you let your gaze fall upon?
Who was witness to your prowess?
Was it glorious?"

<WHERE WAS I? I WAS AT WAR, DOMINIC!
WHERE ELSE SHOULD I BE?>

Of course, the Waker chuckles to himself.
His attention turns to the workers,
moving about the Machine, trying to repair the battle damage.
Complaining, they pull at hydraulic lines.

One mechanic, with little regard for the Machine,
yanks at a line until it suddenly pulls off,
cursing furiously, oil spewing all over.
The Waker stammers, and anger boils over.

"HOW DARE YOU!" The Waker screams.
"This isn't another Bipedal or cannon,
you have at your hands an ancient hero!
How dare you desecrate his tomb!"

The men turn to look at this frail, little Waker.
But before any could speak,
the Waker bellows louder than anyone knew he could
"Leave us! Leave, now! I shall administer the repairs!"

They scoff and turn,
but slowly meander out the port.
The Waker bends over to pick up a wrench,
and rushed over to close off the leak.

<DOMINIC. CALM YOURSELF.
I WILL ENDURE.>

"But my Lord, I must fix you!
You're all over the floor!"

Alone now, the young man immediately
regrets his rash outburst,
his emotions the cause of the next few hours
being turned into calibration and maintenance.

The Waker begins to work on the machinery.
Even breaks out a manual that is so old,
it was actually written on pressed paper
with dried ink. Ancient!

The Juggernaught remains patient,
remains awake as the Waker works.

"My Lord, forgive me,
I know I am keeping you
from you holy, earned slumber.
I should have not ushered those men out."

<NONSENSE! YOU DID WHAT YOU THOUGHT WAS RIGHT.
YOU STOOD FOR SOMETHING. YOU FOUGHT FOR IT.>

Taken aback, the Waker replies,
"Hardly! I didn't throw a single blow.
No one was harmed.
I just... they were treating you low!"

<FIGHTING DOES NOT ALWAYS CONSIST
OF WOUNDING THE ENEMY. CONTINUE TO WORK.>

And so he does.

<DOMINIC.>

The Waker was always flattered that the Juggernaught
refers to him by his name instead of his billet.
Turning wrenches all over while covered in grease and oil,
the young man replies,

"Yes, Marcavius?"

<I HAVE HAD EIGHTEEN WAKERS. OF ALL OF THEM,
YOU ARE THE MOST STRONG.
YOU VIE TO KNOW ABOUT LIFE AND DEATH.
YOU DO NOT STOP BY WHAT YOU ARE LIMITED BY.

EVEN THOUGH OTHERS WILL HOLD YOU BACK.
YOU PUSH. I KNOW THIS, FOR I WAS THE SAME.>

The Waker is speechless.

<LET US SPEAK OF HEROES PAST.
SO THAT THEY THEMSELVES MAY ENDURE.>

"Yes," the Waker says softly.

"Let us speak of their lives and destiny."

<DESTINY? IT IS WAR. WAR IS OUR DESTINY.>"

*Free form poetry at its basis. No meter, little flow. I want to create an image, I want to take you there. Not my usual writing style. Not strict enough for a classic poem, not free enough for plain fiction. This is barely poetry.*

*There will be more of the 1st War Machine and its blur of existence.*

# 54 THE MEDAL

"Bowing as low as he could,
the Knight stoops down from his waist,
bending almost so low his balance was questioned,
only to gracefully straighten back up like a tree.

The silent chamber was teeming with breath,
filled to the brim with the entire battalion
observing their captain be presented his award.
For surely, the King will grant him a medal!

The Knight's own mind was far from present,
being ever so far away from his own presence
as it is when he is in battle.
Like a spectator to his own life.

And in this state,
such a state sought out by seers and wizards alike,
the mind starts to float over memories,
from one to the next.

Like a wall lined with tapestries,
each spinning their own tale,
and spinning ones gaze all over these memories,
these stills of time and space.

The Knight's mind wanders,
but it is not lost.
And at this moment,
so removed from his own award ceremony,

his thoughts are on the battlefield.
That field he had so supposedly earned his medal,
in what so many observed as an act of bravery.
But he did not feel as such.

The battle was being won,
but his own front of Swordsmen
were not faring so well against enemy Calvary.
His men falling with their swords and spears.

His company surrounded,
with no Pikemen to thwart the threat,
and no Archers to pick off the mounted enemy,
he had come to a conclusion.

He and his men were going to die.

With this realization,
and little hesitation,
he commands his men forward,
to certain annihilation.

He tried to rush to the front,
as if to hasten his fate,
but the entire outcome changed,
due to one grave mistake.

The Knight had fell.

Not due to death, but root.
And with his graceless trip,
landing hard on his side,
he falls onto his sword,

and slashed himself a gash.

Picking his head up,
in the midst of the battle din,
the Calvary was seen to strike down his men,
leaving none but ten.

The small circle they made,
around the Knight who had yet to stand,
tightened by the tips of steel,
slowly pressing them in,

before pressing into shield and skin.

All men cried out
before falling with a thud,
covering the Knight with lifeless limbs,
soaking him with warm, red blood.

But before a fate could befall the captain
covered by the bodies of his troops,
a roar is heard over the hillside,
as all forces rush to decimate the enemy.

While enemy horseman were slaying his company,
the rest of his army had won,
who now rushed to pick off the remaining opposing forces,
surrounded in the middle of the valley.

Nowhere was there to run to,
there was nowhere to be led.
The Knight recognized this and burst up,
completely covered in red.

The enemy was decimated,
but everyone had seen their own myth.
The Knight! He was the hero of his company,
the only one to live!

He was covered in the blood of his foes!
He had slayed countless enemy!
He was the last man standing!
He was as heroic as he was deadly!

And he was brought back to his Kingdom,
the Knight who could not die.
Praise to us, for in our midst,
A hero! A Champion!

But the Knight hearts sinks.

He was no hero,
he had settled for death,
and sent his men to die
with not a drop of dignity left.

So with surprise,
returning back to the moment,
he looks down to see,
the most prestigious award ever given.

"I present, to our Champion,
the Medal of David,
for such absolute bravery,
and complete disregard for himself!"

The hall bursts into cheer,
applause ringing of the stone walls,
as the King turns the Knight to face the crowd.
Such a happy moment for the Kingdom.

Such a dark moment for the warrior.
Tears welled up in his eyes,
as he was pulled through the crowd to walk among the village below.
Everyone was oblivious to his apparent sadness.

His denial of his actions,
his guilt of his survival,
his regret for not explaining the truth,
his feelings about the glory he stole.

See him walk, among the soldiers and people,
with a daunting fear of his sleep,
where, with grief, he will be forever punished,
by the medal he gets to keep."

## 55 DETOXIFICATION

"So many in this world today
blur about their day
to get to that one release.
To reach that one buzz.

So popularly seen,
so readily taken,
a way we should deal with our strife,
or celebrate our life.

So many of us had partaken,
to levels beyond repair,
only to regret the haze
the next morning or day.

And yet so few
tend to realize its poison,
or the negativity it can spawn,
like spiders crawling from a web.

Some use it to escape their pain,
finding solace in the bottom of a bottle.
Some people like the way it feels,
filling their fingers with a weight,

a veil behind their eyes,
and a slow smile that creeps upon the lips.
Faded, so many drink to attain this level,
that fine line of freedom that it grants.

But one drop over such amount
always overflows the cup,
for one drink turns to two more
and spills down the slippery slope of control.

Time and time again I slid down this hill,
falling head over heels into a black abyss
I would wake up from the next morning,
my throat sore, my head throbbing.

Time and time again I watched what it did to my life,
I watched relationships tested and torn,
I watched friendships ended,
and opportunities slipped through fingers

as she let go of the hold on my hand.
Time and time again,
all it did was poison my life.
I had no say in its path.

That path that others enjoy,
and use, and live,
but for me it was a wrath
of mistakes and words that never happened.

At the end of this abyss,
one finds the bottom,
through a few solemn nights
of staring at my wall.

But my walls were never empty,
things forgotten were remembered,
a personal quote was taken
and a new life was brewed.

The lack of a toxin,
I so proudly poured down my mouth,
slowly became apparent
with the help of my mentors.

People in my life
made it their goal
to live in the weights,
concerned only with the lift.

The lift of the barbell,
the lift of the cable.
No longer was the lift of the bottle
something of which I was able.

One morning, I woke up,
but instead of the dark pain of the nights alcohol,

I had a soreness in the body
that was only warmed up by the hearth.

The fire of self-betterment,
the test of chipping away,
like a smith at the anvil,
banging flat the sword.

I pushed my body to its limits;
no more would alcohol seep out of my pores,
but instead,
the hard work put into my mornings.

Days turned into weeks,
weeks blurred into months,
and no longer was the bottle desired.
No longer was the poison wanted.

I never saw it as a self-righteous path,
for this was only my journey I decided to take.
And no one was expected to join me
against their own grain or wake.

Not many would follow,
but many would complement,
some would have questions
and all would think...

The detoxification could be painful;
even lengthy.
And most would spurn the event away,
chasing their hangover with another drink.

But all will recognize,
no matter their reasons to consume;
the feeling of being free of such toxins,
even brief, is one most look forward to.

Temptation is abundant,
always wearing a friendly face.
And though I always share the experience,
the drink I now won't partake.

Today I am free,
having been so for a year.
Weakness grows from idleness,
and so, I persevere."

*I use to be a drunken fool, wandering around downtown, trying to drink the city dry. Often it was such an acceptable characteristic to have due to the culture of the Barracks life, the way so many seem to think we should all be on the weekends. Even to those who expect it from me, who seem to always want a drink themselves, drinking was nothing detrimental. Just one drink wasn't bad. But so many times I watched, literally in my face, how that always turned into something negative. Punches thrown, relationships ending over 2 AM phone calls. I had to drag so many people back to their rooms, dealing with so much drama, only to have a sheepish apology the next morning followed by a "wait, I did what?"*

*I was that person for a while, and that was something I did not like. So I removed it from my life, and there was nothing but positive consequences because of it.*

*I do not care that others drink. And for some, that's hard to believe. I sit and watch people partake very often. But at the end of the day, I have no issues knowing the next morning I won't have regrets due to one too many drinks.*

# 56 FRANTIC

"Spinning around,
arms flailing at his sides,
the boy sees too much to focus on
in the playground he has found himself in.

Too excited, his energy is sparking.
You can almost see the hyper energy
fly out his fingertips.
Like a sugar rush gone wrong.

His hands shaking,
he can't contain himself.
Jumping up and around the toys,
the bars that swing.

Hanging off only one hand,
swaying with all his weight,
the sensation that coursed through his veins
was a newfound high.

But the grip that held
onto the bar above his head,
lost its strength like its focus,
and suddenly there was flight.

So much distance was carried,
the momentum making it so,
and the boy lands roughly
against the concrete below.

A pain he had never realized,
much else had been experienced,
burst from his knee
like the blossoming red flower on his trouser.

The squeal of surprise comes
just seconds before the tears,
and then the rising yell belts out of the mouth
of the injured youth.

And he cries, this boy,
hands shaking, face red,
frantic for a source of comfort
that was nowhere to be found.

The boy cried and cried,
but there was no one to scoop up the pain,
and no way to quell the storm
which spun in his head.

He cried so hard he lost his voice,
which scared him even more.
So he stopped a moment
and took in a deep breath.

The original reason was to belt a louder yell,
but instead of more anger,
the sudden halt brought a new sensation.
The opposite of what he was fluttering all afternoon in.

Taking in another breath,
this one deeper than the last,
he finds a new game,
of how long he can keep this new feeling.

His heart rate falls,
as does the rage he had at life.
The pain ebbs away,
his tears began to dry.

Breathing deep,
he holds it in,
to see how long he could,
and if he could increase the wait.

The boy finds a new way,
in the span of a play in the park,
to deal with life.
He does not know it.

But some spend their whole lives
trying to discover a way to cope.
When life seems all but worth it,
without a single ray of hope.

Take heed, the boy would be wise to do,
for taking a second to gain a moment,
and losing what is seen as frantic
will spare his days less tears.

Less pain. Not less blood,
for that always flows.
But sadness can be corked.
And this fact, the boy now knows."

# 57 THE GIFT

"From the mountains,
to the trees.
From the hill side,
to the seas.

There's this place,
I long to be.
If I could show you,
would you come with me?

Just look at it all,
just where we are.
We have enough light,
from the Moon and Stars.

Just breathe and take it in all in.

This is a gift,
right where we stand.
This moment in time,
has everything at hand.

The grass beneath our feet,
the Earth cool on our toes.
The air that surrounds us
carries away our woes.

It's so easy to miss
the flowing and warm vibes.
But anyone can learn to feel them,
if you only take the time.

Breathe. And take it in.

Twice more will we say,
the beauty that we all have imbued,
so take my hand, and let me lead,
away from the view so skewed.

We all can see light,
for we all have it in us.
It's bright when the sun gets low,
reflecting off the leaves and dust.

You seem so wired,
but there's a burning desire,
to fold in, and crush such stones,
look in your heart and you'll find home.

Breathe. Take it in.

The land is a gift,
but so is our time.
From the wind on our faces,
that tickle wind chimes,

to the smiles we share,
making us share one heart.
There is truly nothing that keeps
happiness and our lives apart.

That is the gift,
the weightlessness of joy.
The secret is realizing,
it's one inhale away.

Breathe."

# 58 ILLUSTRIOUS

"I am not forever, I will die.
I will pass to dust, and even the memories
that associate my life with my name
will fade into oblivion.

But the fabled old of heroes bold
are forever. Legion, are our tales;
the whispers of enemies' fears
and children's prayers. We few.

Sunlight riders, night raiders,
we descend upon those who affront our existence.
Those who wish us the ill will,
we quiet their lives with a definitive finish.

But to become one with such power,
we fall onto the ground in such groveling.
Those who wish to grasp at the Title
step into position to begin training.

We hone our bodies; we break our minds.
But rather than mindless, we sharpen our will,
for steel sharpens steel. We lose all grasps
of our old lives and are taught anew.

In the youngest days of our boyhoods
we run together, eat together,
sweat together, and bleed together.
Having not an ounce of imagination of what was next.

Every day was a surprise, a death run,
a new class, a punishment,
all geared to making us stronger.
What seemed detrimental was helpful.

But the best part was the history.
The glorious, illustrious history!
Battles spanning from every clime and place,
to the tactics that changed history.

Single heroes, charging the enemy with one weapon,
others putting their back to death,
while bringing wounded back home.
The bravest the world has seen.

This morning, I honored such a man. Humbled.
In the midst of us alive today,
one such warrior led his own
on the beaches of death.

Storming the sands of unknown lands,
this legend ran to and fro,
with a much deeper connection
with the ones to his left and right.

In times where his skin led others to hate,
to detest this man on diabolical terms,
over a hatred so disgusting, yet
taught to the youth of that day.

A shameful time for his land,
this man was discriminated,
and segregated. But instead of kneeling down;
he stood up and answered the call.

In the time where his nation was at war,
he left his home, his friends,
and family. For a new life to begin
he stood in line at Montford point.

This man trained as hard as others,
and most likely harder, it seems.
He rightfully earned the title
of United States Marine.

Like I had done, many years later.
This man went to war,
and fought for his country,
and came home to fight another.

He watched the hands of time spin,
and the laws of man change the nation.
He watched grips loosen,
and the Corps changed to a more tolerant place.

Soon, this man saw other men,
and women, to be sure,
join the God blessed Corps
that shared his ancestry.

Free from subjugation
of the segregation
he had seen test
his motivation, dedication.

This man, and his fellow unit,
lead the way for others to serve.
To give his life for a country
at the time so ungrateful, hateful.

But today, the nation as a whole,
in lieu of its elected Congress
voted unanimously to award such a man
with the highest honor it can bestow.

The Congressional Gold Medal
was awarded to Corporal Jesse James Henderson.
A man who my fellow Marines
will always give thanks.

Regardless of skin, race, color,
and many more adjectives I can name,
we stand on his shoulders,
and the shoulders of every Marine before us.

Like the long list of recruits
who had stood on the exact yellow footprints I stepped on.
Who had later became Marines. War fighters.
Heroes, legends, fables.

The most important thing we commit to memory
is the illustrious history
of my beloved Corps.
It will always live on.

I am nothing. Almost hiding from thanks.
I feel so unworthy of gratitude and handshakes.
But the man so spoken highly about
deserves all such praise, and so much more.

He is one of the few,
our history lends its tongue to.
Where we lend our ears, and in doing so,
our hearts grow with pride.

I will die. I am a United States Marine.
Though I will perish,
The Marine Corps will live on.
The Marine Corps is forever.

And so, I am forever!
All the lives I have touched,
will always pass down about the Corps.
As the Corps that was passed down to me.

Because of men like Cpl. Henderson,
and a list that deserves more
than my meek attempt at the written word.
I will live on.

They paint the wide history of the Corps
with the colors that evoked me to join.
Every day in my life, I try to pay homage
to the heroes I look up to.

Battles that can be read as future wars with xenos.
Marches across lands so alien to our world.
Untold moments of the evil of man,
and the strength of the spirit.

If art is how we decorate space,
and music is how we decorate time,
let the story of Montford Point
paint its tale in your mind.

I am proud
to claim the title
United States Marine.
Let that sink in."

# 59 NARROWED EYES

"The creak of the door
breaks the silence that ebbed at me.
And with it, the change of focus
expels from the glass in my hand.

Towards the frame,
bursting through the frame,
was a presence so heavy
it knocked my sense of space.

Time seemed to slow as she walked,
one delicate boot stepping onto the wooden floor.
My gaze swallowed every inch
of her flow, a perfect transition of weight.

I watched her legs glide one past another,
jeans neatly wrapped, so tight.
Tucked into the boots that sounded her entrance
with the clack of heels that always steals my attention.

She hasn't even made it past the Open sign,
yet she has everyone staring all over.
She isn't clad without class,
obviously she picked her outfit with care.

A burgundy shirt draped her slight frame,
giving some clarity to what she was gifted with.
For most of us, it was a gift indeed.
Voluptuous, if you want to be vulgar.

Her waist and hips differed much in width,
giving the hourglass a run for its money.
A full shape that was so pleasant to look at as a whole,
or treat to stare at one portion.

Her hair complimented her threads,
a dirty, rusty blonde giving off her brown and red clothes a glow.
Freckles and glasses led my thoughts to her eyes,
and I was half expecting blinding beauty.

But before I could see such eyes,
she was too far, having walked to the counter.
What an intoxicating feeling,
to have her in my sight. So I stand.

Walking up to the girl,
I start to feel less impressed by her gorgeous space.
The air is so heavy,
and I began to doubt what is what.

Leaning onto the counter beside,
I feel annoyance as she turns her head,
and a judging glare that burns up and down
my all-of-a-sudden lacking image.

I look down myself after her smirk,
noticing all too well the holes in my shorts,
the age of my shirt, the only saving grace
newer shoes that had been given to me graciously.

I look up again, and see narrowed eyes,
such a gaze that makes me realize
that I am doing nothing but wasting her time.
Such ridiculous thoughts, that I should speak to her a line.

I sit, embarrassed,
only to watch her stride out of the door,
no enjoyment in watching her leave
as it all winks goodbye at me.

What a fool, I was,
to think I even had a chance.
Frustrating, I think to myself,
and look back down to my glass.

This coffee is warm still,
as is my blood. My day
is shining still. The Sun
is above, giving light to my life.

So why should I feel so crushed?
I shouldn't. There are worse things,
for at least I draw breath, deeply.
I can see, in her eyes.

She wanted something I wasn't,
and maybe I'm not that much as is.
But she wanted a completely different man,
and that is reason enough for withdrawal.

That I couldn't fill her skies,
or even reach them. But lies,
only lies, would gain me any ground.
Only when they became true,

would it be too late to know,
that though I lost her,
I was such a fool.
To even try to fill up her eyes.

My glass in front of me is empty.
That's what's now.
I forget what was past,
and enjoy the glass I have."

# 60 POSTER BOY

"I'm trying, I really am.
I feel so loose right now.
My shoes aren't tied tight,
like a loose nut rattling off a bolt.

My head is all over the place,
my mind bobbing from one memory to another.
One second of thinking of the beach,
being swept by it to the bed I used to lay in.

Then to a desert, one I hated to know,
its grains of sands switching to the dirt on my pants.
Bits of clay sticking to my knee from my fall,
the misuse of balance a main aggravator.

I can't even concentrate at the task at hand,
so uncomfortable in the accusation of an easy life.
As though I rub that dirty towel in the face of others,
like I don't know hardship, what it does.

Do not preach to me about pain! Are you serious?
God, my blood boils. Like a child who doesn't comprehend.
My fists shake with so much anger,
This is what it comes to. Loss.

And it doesn't matter,
the feeling of falling that I feel.
The examination of such emotion is left to the imaginary,
for no one will wonder about my plight.

Pity the plight of young fellows,
as they wander about in regret.
Pity the plight of young fellows,
and their anxious attempt to forget.

What a write off,
the misguided opinions of distaste,
that crush back down on the land
I have always left without walls.

Feels like playing with fire.
It doesn't burn the first time.
Your hand walks through the flame.
But it's bitter and sweet; scorching skin.

One day I'll learn, when I've been burned.
But I still don't know the lesson,
as I sit like a child just scolded
over an unintelligible crime.

So frustrating, the automatic disdain,
now look at this.
He's beating up his only friend,
the one who gave him money for the pen.

The older boys don't care,
even though only a snake acts like that.
But what difference does it make
as long as someone fell for the trap.

I don't have age on my side,
never did, never will,
only fed lies inside
and I'm not going to listen.

I've already made my decision.
In the field of choice,
may have already lost the proposition.
And now I'm just another poster boy

for the broken men
of my generation.

So to fall to such accusations?
Shall I live the life of a joke?"

*A sad day.*

# 61 HAMMERHEAD

"It must move forward,
it must always push.
A lack of progress
would cause slow death.

Though indeed, time is the champion,
and we're all the challengers,
just to survive
the beast must swim.

Feared by many, sought out by few,
respected and hated by all.
Power and grace comes to mind as it glides,
cutting through the Ocean depths.

Disregarded as brainless,
maybe only ruled by primal tendencies,
the path it takes along its life
lead from one meal to another.

Always moving.
Not lost,
but wandering out its life
in an effort to make the inevitable tardy.

For the beast has no way
to push life through its body,
save the forward motion of swimming on,
of never standing still.

Weakness grows from idleness,
and with this hunter it's an understatement,
because it can't breathe without this phenomenon.
It must swim, or die.

Constantly swimming,
sometimes missing a meal or two,
not stopping to enjoy any moment,
the shark is on a never ending mission.

An ever-updating objective,
from one to the next,
not sitting to think about the day.
Not able to meditate on his life.

His life unrecorded,
save the chance encounters of those
that keep it to negative lights.
But it is never envious.

It never wishes to be like us,
it never says it wants to be one of us,
it just lives. A shark does not question life.
It swims and kills and dies.

Sometimes I wonder what it would be like.
With no one to love me,
no one to love back. No one to hate,
No one to hate who I am.

Instead, I would move. I would swim,
to keep from drowning,
I would dash from one meal to the next.
I would not sit and try to write my soul out.

I would not feel heartache,
I would could not spread my views of life or death,
positive vibes or negative lifestyles,
smell the roses or watch the seasons.

I would not know right from wrong,
evil from good,
I would lose all my love for things,
the Ocean and the Sun.

I sometimes feel like a shark,
a hammerhead swimming along,
just pushing through to survive,
without really living.

Love is the answer,
I know this to be true.
There isn't a big secret,
just an unpopular facet to feel.

We must exercise love
by forgiving one another,
give out hands to help
instead of receive.

Love is the answer,
there is no other,
Life's true meaning.
The thing that carries us through.

I don't know if you feel like this, too,
but I haven't gills that adorn my neck.
I breathe deep, I swim along,
maybe it's time I balance the notes.

World of music,
just be nice and maintain the space.
I do not want to push out disgrace.
I do not throw words and hope it sticks.

Let the Lion roar,
let the Sheep run.
Let the Shark swim,
let me live one."

# 62 NIGHT AND DAY

"Moon Child, Moon Child,
where are you off to now?
Always a night away,
but never the same phase.

I lay to rest my head,
it spinning about another,
no other.
My hearts beating like a drum,

in reggae rhythm,
so strong, like the Sun above.
No matter the clouds,
it always shines.

Then my conduit sets,
the last rays dancing on the hills,
before it paints the sky the upper Chakras
and gives way to the darker half.

His other half,
the Sun and His gorgeous Moon.
The Moon and Her glorious Sun.
Her opposite.

Impossible,
to hold them together,
yet they are never far apart.
They both shine on us.

The Sun is my idol,
always bright, pushing positivity,
life-giving light unto me.
Shining on face and skin, growing smiles.

The Sun gives us life,
alongside our Earth. I respect and praise both,
we should all love and protect all.
Give thanks to all we have.

The Sun is constant,
easy to follow,
giving light to my life
and the path I try to walk.

The pure, righteous,
holy white it burns onto me,
pushes me from green to blue,
my Ocean and all her wrath.

The Earth's own vibe made manifest,
the Oceans swells me high and low.
Yet She is pulled by the Lady above.
Like I seem to be pulled to you.

This is no love poem,
but an observation on the similarities
and the differences.
The difference of cycles

and the phases, or lack thereof.
The push of energy,
the drawing of our own lights.
And the view on our lives.

The Moon I do not know,
never having spent time to learn,
but what she does to my Ocean
has always evoked my smile.

Your New, naked Moon
pushes the water higher
giving spring tides to wave riders
along with the glory of the Full show.

Your Half-Moon nips back the water,
pulling less on the blanket
as the Earth pulls her sheets back
and granting us neap tides.

But we all rise,
as I am pulled back and forth through all phases
and the energy that we share,
giving back and forth.

The Moon embraces the Sun,
the Sun lends Her a white dress.
Is that why I am glad to hear from you
all night and day?

No need to question
the path we travel
for it's the same
that has been treaded since time.

To us, granted the Sun
with His warmth at day,
and the Moon
with Her vibes at night.

Just a pull of one on the other."

# 63 WRITTEN WORD

"An analysis, often forgotten,
in this world of written word,
is the actual act of writing.
Pouring heart with pencil and pen.

Having watched technology grow
in front of me, exponentially,
my use for the pen and pad
has become limited to work.

Such pleasure is taken,
spilling now my thoughts in ink,
and looking at my sloppy
handwriting. Chicken scratch.

But if poetry is words
of a writers truest soul,
then my own handwriting
is my soul's accent.

Others who write, cleaner,
maybe have a crisper voice!
They have a beautiful soul,
shown by hand and words alike.

I cannot transfer this,
onto screen of limits,
our phones and webpages
turning me into one less intouch.

So listen, well, read, reader:
Write a poem. See it grow,
turn into a heartfelt prose.
Or letter, or declaration.

This you read now, an attempt
at explaining the feeling
of writing my soul out...
is lacking. But still an attempt."

# 64 A PUSH TO THE LEFT

"I tried to lie,
lying in my bed and telling myself
that I shouldn't be up before 8.
That inside these sheets I should hide.

Yeah, right.
Just like the advice
I chose to ignore
to stay out late to celebrate.

I celebrate life way different,
a fresh air movement,
a way that some see too loose
for the man I think I am.

I just don't have the time
to wait on slowpokes,
my personified life
jumping back and forth between too many things.

Like this piece,
words trailing from one to the next,
but each moment one I do enjoy,
thank you; just not like you all.

Belligerent is the tone,
I got a random hair that spills me around town,
with love on my mind but a desire in my heart,
they could never keep us apart.

The Ocean, of course.
Her push onto my face are memories,
miles away, but still crisp
as the first wave that broke to my right.

I went left,
rode that wave as far as I could,
a smile on my lips and a laugh climbing out my throat,
like a goblin laughing in glee.

Cackling, if you will.
Goofy, like my push to the left,
my left foot pushing me along
these gray seas with right foot forward.

Goofy being backwards,
childish, even,
either falling into a goof troupe
or building my own.

Always spinning out something,
I have something for everyone.
A jack of all trades, a master of none,
I can talk your shirt off, like mine already is.

Athletic? Sure,
but let the glasses be the tale,
giving character to my face,
reflecting my stellar grades.

Scholastics was a joke,
I nailed it like a carpenter,
but my woodwork was saturated
with the world of science fiction.

Never been normal,
not this early bird,
as I'm up and at, well,
the world as we all know it.

The nerd against the world,
though what makes me a nerd,
except my love for all things
considered weird and lame.

Mythos, I suppose,
it entertains me.
Plus other things,
as is the never ending pursuit.

Pursuit of happiness,
pursuit for the perfect wave,
having stalled by my pursuit
for the carve that feels the same.

I may or may not have had it in my grasp,
the one and only,
the one I thought was perfect
the one who saw me so high.

But I was on the shoulder of the wave,
I paddled too late for it,
I was cut off,
it passed right under me.

Or maybe I was scared?
I always push to my left,
when most people ride right.
And that wave was such a great ride,

but lost to my hesitation.
So now I rise,
earlier than ever before
to catch another wave.

Surfboard,
longboard,
mat in the studio
or bench in the Mecca.

These I need,
but will it be enough for the push?
The desire to better myself
burns ever so bright.

Maybe it will falter.
They say the stars that burn the brightest
will extinguish first.
Am I doomed to a listless fate?

Let that light shine, I say,
scattered more left than right,
my left side the weaker,
but always my go-to.

The functionality is weaker,
but I'd rather wipeout
than lose another ride.
Terms blurred,

this piece in pieces,
like other parts of me.
But my resolve?
Like the mountain I now live on."

# 65 SERVICE

"To serve is its own reward.

In the idea of man,
and our fathomable demise,
will you strive to give your life to others?

Without Dark, there can be no Light.

Not in consequence of your breath,
but your sweat,
your tears, your blood, even.

Without the Lie, there can be no Truth.

How far would you go to serve?
Would you lay your pride down,
to grasp the handles of the load of another?

Without the Loss, there can be no Sacrifice.

There are lengths
so uncomfortable it's considered foolish,
that people will go.

Without Despair, there can be no Hope.

To serve what they believe in.
To pass down the torch,
handed down unto us as a light of legacy.

Without War, there is no Peace.

Let the war wage. Any war.
And war is not limited to steel and blood.
Mind and soul fight and die every day.

To serve is to give,
to go unappreciated,
to not have your receiving hand out,
the fingers having withdrawn.

It can be as vague, or as big,
as the years of service to a cause,
or as specific and small
as buying the thirsty man a drink.

The difference between gifting and service
is not the money spent,
nor the intention behind it,
but the base emotion.

Gifting is out of love,
or perhaps something ulterior,
but service is out of pride,
out of honor, a thirst to see an end.

Seek not glory,
glory begets arrogance.
Seek not retribution,
for nobody owes you anything.

Open minds can be seen as weak,
as is tolerance for the opposite end.
The only worse thing than a heretic is a traitor.
The only difference is ignorance.

A closed mind is a well-guarded mind,
protected from wavering thoughts.
Resolve becomes doctrine,
doctrine becomes action.

Find a cause,
go out and serve.
Serve your fellow man,
serve something more.

Those who claim no instruction?
Ignorance is a virtue.
And ignorance is no excuse.
You must succeed.

Success is commemorated;
failure only remembered.
Success is measured in blood;
yours or the enemy's.

Service without deeds is worthless,
but servitude with acts big and small
and no payment
is the purest form of a rich life.

Give in to your cause,
and lead the waging war.
In what way is there to earn more?
To serve is its own reward."

# 66 DESPAIR

"Need something to numb the pain,
feels like I'm falling out of the run.
Maybe I already did,
watching others race past.

The heat is heavy on me,
pushing me to exhaustion,
but it is more than my body
that seems to be crumbling.

What a despicable moment,
this instance of falling.
It feels like I have no one to turn to,
and with all this support, loneliness.

The tears well up,
the eyes become murky,
rather, my sight,
as I fall to the ground on this run called life.

Such an unwanted misstep,
and look what it's caused,
scrapped knees and lost dreams,
at least that how it feels.

No! It wasn't supposed to be like this,
this must be a nightmare.
Like a flashing strobe,
snapping me images at the nightclub.

But instead of dancing to the beat,
I feel like crying,
and maybe I will.
Or already did.

I feel like there is no hope,
crushing is this despair
that doesn't rule my life
but has latched its teeth deep.

They're sinking into skin,
and it burns...
I want something to numb it,
so I become numb.

Going about my day in a haze,
maybe muttering 'I'm fine',
but maybe I am.
I don't know.

I think I just need to let my heart escape,
maybe for just one day,
because either way I'll keep breathing,
this heart keeps beating.

No smiles,
the day is still gray
but my eyes see bright,
dry and blue.

I'll just stay true,
let my heart lead,
it'll lend me joy
as I make it through

this little despair.
I've been through harder!"

# 67 SOME DIFFERENCES BETWEEN TWO LOVERS

"The way she awakens
I have witnessed many times.
She is a glorious sight,
after a full, fruitful night,

laying in the sheets,
hair all about,
skin exposed to the air,
though this time it's alabaster, not brown.

Having left one bed
and slipped into another,
these sheets are thicker,
for here it's colder in the morning.

I lazily rise,
for no surf to run to,
nor Mecca that has open doors.
I dress and then watch her wake.

Night and Day
are always so different.
The smells, the colors,
contrast fully like a photo negative.

This time around,
watching her rise for the first time,
varies different from the one I used to coax awake,
this one seems to wake herself.

Somewhat.
Either way,
I'm fully dressed,
moving about my morning already.

The sun isn't as bursting here,
so less yellows are poking
through the windows.
But this one is just as warm to hold.

The air still bites,
sending my own skin to goose bumps,
but now having a warm embrace from this new acquaintance,
I warm up.

Though the smell of salt
is not in the air, only in my head,
and the blue of the Ocean nowhere near,
my morning outside is graced with green.

More so than the last,
these two differ so much.
But I would be completely lying
if I said I didn't still love the one left behind.

God I love her, she knows it, too.
Though I have to say, this one...
the one currently waking up in front of me...
I am growing to enjoy.

This one has so much to enjoy,
from a very different stand point.
From walking around in my haze
to pushing along the sidewalk.

The ride is different,
these streets less busy.
San Diego wakes up
so different from Chattanooga."

# 68 NEW AGE FEEL

"The pounding into my ears
reminds me of war drums,
but instead of pushing fear into my veins
it gives me nerve to push harder.

And now I glide,
the day still dry,
the streets giving way to the wheels
that make the ride into that of the Sea.

No, this isn't another piece
to express how my soul feels
about the passion I have
for my boards or waves.

Or the combination of the two.
Rather, a relapse in memory
of the lives I have lived
and the return of some aspects.

Facets, little portions,
considering I'm too multi-faceted.
For others. But in my eyes,
just the building blocks that make me up.

Like a well-conceived model
put together with Legos that don't match.
The attempt to grow up fast.
Wearing expensive clothes don't make you a man.

It's late and I'm staring at the ground,
thoughts of Seattle city streets
filling my head;
all the times I snuck out from my Mom's house.

A second story window was hard to slip through
at first. Just like the first time
I ran with the big kids,
who told me what clothes to wear.

Graphic tees, dark hoodies,
to not draw attention.
But that's not how a youth should think;
not when there's kites to fly.

So fly I did.
Growing out of the troubled years
of my younger teenage numbers
and instead gave back to young ones.

And then moving on
to give even more,
time to get away from the rain and clouds,
letting my Legacy lead me on.

Five generations,
almost hard to believe,
but only after three months
it was meant to be.

A boy becomes a boy,
thinking he was a man;
his mannerisms fibbing to the world
he could handle business of adults.

What is an adult?
I don't know. I skate,
my head is swimming in waves more than anyone
could even guess, more than one could know.

I can see the Sun come up.
Water never felt this good.
Air never felt this pure.
Does the past matter right now?

It feels like life is taking over,
it feels like it's meant to be.
I can feel the Earth beneath my feet,
I can feel the Stars press down on me.

Things have never looked so clear,
things that have been said to me
make more sense, given thought,
pushing me to clarity.

The push I always talk about,
the voice inside my head
that usually is so live.
Lately has been so quiet.

Not much instruction forthcoming.
But now I don't feel so lost.
No, I'm not healed from a wound,
for there was no strike.

No, I'm not enlightened,
for I've barely begun on that journey,
but I'll tell you right now,
right now,

I can feel the Sun rays dance on me,
I can feel the Moon pull on the Sea,
I can feel the Earth underneath my feet,
I can feel the Stars press down on me.

I can feel it's meant to be."

# 69 EQUAL PARTS

"Two ounces espresso,
two ounces steamed.
On what kind of milk, I'm not certain,
though I am sure it isn't almond.

Two cortados,
delicately placed,
made with passion instead,
for me by the newlywed.

Her company; enjoyable,
Mannerisms; adorable,
the light of her mood
matching my ever positive vibe.

Two drinks,
equal parts,
to be enjoyed by two lovers,
who make each other whole.

On their own, a treat,
each a different roast,
their own characteristics
dancing different jigs on my palate.

But together,
so crisp,
each drink
complementing the other.

Alas! No one to share,
and a second too late the newlywed noticed,
at the outcome of these drinks
only to be enjoyed by one.

No equal part,
no pair I partake in,
no other half
that makes my blend.

The difference,
fresh love, and the lack thereof,
spills both equal
into the cup of the day.

Though the drink isn't bitter,
no salt spoil the mix,
a simple laugh and a wave
downplay the hidden sadness.

One drink swallowed,
and another pushed down,
both drinks so good,
but enjoyed by one.

Only one,
the other, not aware,
nor a care perhaps,
of the espresso not shared.

Both cortados,
equally as good,
purchased and drank,
make the night more live.

As the heart sinks a little."

# 70 GREY WAVE

"Foot on board,
fear erupts from the volcano
that is suddenly
echoing its wrath in my stomach.

The pit of the gut,
to be accurate. Now,
coming up only to be pushed back
by a gulp of anxiety.

The wave is massive.
I have yet to catch a wave
like one which waited before me.

It isn't moving,
this one I don't need to paddle
out of its way.
But I must move.

Down this slab?
The face is ridiculous,
but the rush isn't measured
by the feet of the crest.

The Wave is in front of me,
beckoning me to go.
But I stand planted,
fellow wave riders waiting behind.

This is a series I haven't watched,
a show I am unfamiliar with.
These waves are unforgiving,
there will be no cushion for error.

Gloves on tight,
board wheels tightened,
I push slowly,
and as my nose dives down

my speed picks up.
Faster, faster,
but no left to take.
No other surfers to avoid.

This hill is crazy,
and my legs shake from fear,
but I lean over,
hands behind back.

No good reason,
this being so inconsequential.
But maybe I can join this crowd.
This Downhill Division.

I have bitten into waves,
having been smashed by Her might
of thousands of years of Ocean
 among the shores.

But here on Mother Earth,
manmade tracks,
concrete waves,
grey seas,

scare me. Rock me,
to my core,
like the fall that racks my body
and my limbs and joints.

Board flies past,
I peel myself off the ground,
the rush having blurred the wave I just caught
into a searing memory to keep.

The Ocean calls to me,
I must answer her wail.
To catch a wave
is to be on top of the world.

So I try to mount these.
Let the new wrath take me.
Grind me, like stones
crushing stones.

Let me lose myself
to the Seas.
Blue or Grey,
they help me cope.

Loss, regret,
pain, suffering.
Hatred, frustration,
jealousy. Seething Fury.

The Seas wash it away."

*A newfound hobby, in an attempt to recapture the rush of surfing.*

# 71 FAMILIES

"Families have never been limited
by blood or last names. For me,
if I want to be specific,
it almost has no prerequisites.

Save one, the bond,
the thing that makes us family.
I have so many, so maybe
I am not a good family member?

Sad to think, even with my kin,
I know so little in the extent of them,
though that contrasts highly with
my immediate relatives.

My Mother, my hero,
my Sister, my counterpart,
my Brother, my heart,
but so far away they are.

My other families
don't share birthplace or blood.
but the bond couldn't be stronger.
Actually,

the members come and go.
Some due to time,
some due to orders,
some due to moving on.

Whether that be in life or death.
My other families
sit on different ends of the spectrum.
Vary, they do, in large ways.

My biggest family, the brotherhood
of those put through the forge
and worked on like great metal weapons
until fine steel is produced.

We brothers, the Firing Battery,
the green machine,
we went through hell.
That always makes a bond. Fox Battery.

A bond deeper than blood,
I tend to keep my promises.
Some still cling to another,
but we all are family.

My family, of the ones
who scream down hills,
my newest addition.
Downhill Division.

So close to my fond friends
who us together, brave the Ocean,
started down the journey from
kook to, well, an experienced kook. Us Surfers.

My family of youths,
so long ago that we'd swim,
and I lead, a flag pole in my hand,
the Furious First. Chanting.

The Brash Crowd, regulars,
like myself now, that originally brought me in,
along with the deep breathers
of the Yoga Landing.

They all understand me,
different parts,
make me better
in one way or another.

Do I return the favor?"

# 72 EXPLICIT

"Does it matter what year I was born?
Or what time of the year?
Is it relevant the position of the Sun?
Or the axis of the Earth?

No. Not at all.
Not my sign, that doesn't determine much,
just similarities of things I add up
in my own head.

But what does matter?
I'll show you,
let me show you,
prove how much I'll break you.

To rubble? Goodness, no,
not at all.
To exhaustion maybe.
All from the stroke.

First, let us start with that dress,
or lack thereof,
because once you move it off,
you move me tight, just right,

for every time my eyes lay on you,
exposed, vulnerable,
I'll be taking you in,
cherishing, like it's the first time.

Every time.
Every time I'll kiss every inch,
being sure to press my lips
all over you to drive your senses wild.

So wild, like what is to come.
Only to lay it all out,
lay you down,
make you feel all right.

In all the right places. I'll caress,
with just the fingertips,
sending shivers up and down your spine,
arms, legs. Head, even,
brushing your ears with my breath.

Breaking the anticipation past its capacity,
you can't wait, literally.
For what I can do;
what I would love to do, if you let me.

Maybe, if you are so inclined,
you can decline yourself onto the bed,
or floor. That would be fun,
though either way will be enough.

Enough for me to go down,
not rough,
placing all the attention
to what calls for sweet, succulent sensation.

I'll be sure to lick all points,
every inch in such a manner
of a craftsman, quality man;
making his finest production.

I'll produce, as you have already seen,
driving you so wild
as your fingertips run through my hair,
pulling my head closer,

toes curling,
heels digging into my back,
legs thrown over shoulders,
all surfaces being pressed.

My own hands running up and down,
grasping those two lovelies, as they nearly lie out of reach,
exposed to the world
as you lay on your back.

So much happening,
multiple stimulation,

until you demand I come up for air,
but I take my time kissing up your body,

to your neck. That sweet neck,
pausing to drive you crazy
as I bear down on you,
not menacingly, nor aggressive

but dominant.
I have spent time giving you all for nothing,
and I will not ask the same of you,
but I will place something.

Pleasuring, as it enters,
always slow to start,
everything slowing down,
including the hands of time.

At this point, eyes are locked,
but everything else has no brakes,
all stops are pulled,
quite the downhill rush.

But instead,
I rise up,
sitting up to bring
your body to bear.

Your lower half,
both of those smooth long limbs,
up against my chest,
squeezing you tighter around me.

Much tighter,
every inch felt
during every single stroke.
Your eyes slightly closed,

your lips parted wide.
Your moans permeating the air
along with the heat
of the moment. So long,

but not lasting forever.
Every time,
the climax rushes too fast,
and without control it comes.

Not that we hate that,
especially after the fact.
Laying there,
both covered in a slight sweat,

your head laying on my heart,
your hand still wandering around,
fingertips tip-toeing around my skin.
Our sex gets better every time."

*So yeah.*

# 73 HUMBLING

"Once, while walking,
both of us strolling for caffeine,
this beautiful creature turned,
with confidence, and said to me:

'You won't realize how much you don't know
about cooking until you start to learn and do,'
and thinking back to that,
in my ears her words ring true.

I thought I knew how to cook,
but laughably I was off,
but how do I say this
without diminishing my own effort?

I love to cook,
I love to make creations,
and that moment where a patron takes a bite,
and smiles creep on their faces,

it's so rewarding.
It's what I really want to do,
in the end, to just surf,
grow a garden, cook.

Someone has to make a decision,
it's you. Whether or not to actually do it,
to chase what you truly like to do,
even if you're so caught up

in another way of life.
And so I walk in,
not a lick of experience
save misled intuition.

And so on day one,
having the knife taken away from me,
scolded on the method I had laid
the food out to be cut,

I was humbled in the thing I claimed skill.
But not beaten down,
for being enthusiastic
won me extra attention.

So I am learning,
only having just chipped away
at the very tip of this iceberg.
The intention to bust the whole glacier.

But better more are the ones who eat,
for not everyone may cook,
but everyone loves a good meal,
and that takes no second look.

Friends, people,
shop owners, gun slingers,
phone operators and longboarders,
all request from me some eats,

and I deliver,
only for a couple of days.
But so far my skill, or lack thereof
have gotten me nothing but praise.

So rewarding! Their smiles,
their compliments so kind.
What's somewhat funny is the recipe
that brings the brightest comments,

is one handed down to me by my Mother,
who is native to San Salvador.
The very first thing I made on my own.
When I decided I wanted to cook.

I love to cook. Back in the barracks,
the blocks of artilleryman,
the dip was worked on,
perfected, to a point

that mouths from Lake Forest,
Huntington and Mission Beach,
Seattle and Chattanooga,
and of course, Las Pulgas,

love it.
Off menu, made again in this establishment,
for those to enjoy,
making their meals complimented.

I have so much to learn,
I have definitely been humbled,
but the opposite of a stumble,
I'll be in the kitchen again soon.

Please, place your order."

# 74 A.T.

"A Boy and his Dog,
the both of them bro-gendary.
Every day, they wake,
without care in their tree house.

Given as a gift,
only after being earned in combat,
by the Queen of the Nightosphere,
the radical dame who likes to play games.

They awake, and then the cook of the two,
who made a sandwich once so good,
it stopped time itself (with the help of a man of magic),
makes the two breakfast to fuel their day.

Skateboarding in and out,
the little blue box who wants to be more,
the three rush out to save the day,
any day, that needs saving.

With the sword full of Demons blood,
depending on what episode, though,
The Boy and his Dog run to the Kingdom,
made of sweets and caramel.

The Princess, pretty in pink,
Pee-Bubs, perhaps, sends the heroes off,
for there's trouble in the land of Ice.
It's ruler, a misunderstood King.

Though misunderstood, a menace he is,
kidnapping is not accepted
in this land of the past.
A past forgotten in the future.

Much like his own origins, the Boy,
raised by the family of the Dog,
private investigators, apparently.
The Boy was a stinky baby.

One who was buff,
who could dance like a man.
One who could shake his fanny,
who could shake his can.

Growing up, of course,
with age still not on his side,
the young hero fights with his heart,
like he loves. Fire,

the burning sensation
that fills the boy's head,
a warmth all up inside,
kissing and passing rocks.

The Boy pushes the memory away,
back to the task at hand,
already in battle with the I.K.
The Dog encompassing the field.

So many adventures,
and life times lived,
from all the lessons
this universe gives.

Stories of love,
of heartache,
of misgivings and desires,
of the meaning of life.

Help others, that's what F.T.H. does,
with J.T.D., the fun that never ends.
Though watch out for the one with Lumps,
the sassy one who always crashes parties.

So annoying. Though,
she'll take you to the deep end,
L.S.P. happens to be on life guard duty.
You might get wet.

Or lose your mind,
depending on how much you want to think.
Shoot, look at Prismo's place.
His Time Room bends too many rules, mathematically.

Algebraic!
Seriously,
this show has erected a castle in my heart.
Like Betty leaving Simon for... Simon.

So maybe come along with me.
There's this town besides the Sea that I know.
There's more mountains than forest,
but we can still do so as we please."

# 75 A LITTLE WASTEFUL

"Inconsequential,
or at least trivial,
our lives can be.
And so, too, our desires.

Want versus need,
a dilemma some of us face,
while others hum over the decision
between a meal or a place to sleep.

The car can be driven,
to wherever the driver wants,
if the gas is full,
the destination chosen.

But when that destination is far,
and not a priority for life,
the want takes over,
the money gets spent.

Gas, rather. Spewed,
the pollution is created,
adding the water drop
to the tidal wave of destruction

we envelop this poor place.
Such a waste it is, or was,
driving around to do what?
Just more things not needed?

Yes, at first an idea that was decent,
now an immediate regret,
a want not needed,
an hour I'll never get back.

An experience I missed out on,
for who knows what could have happened
during that time that passed
in this wonderful thing called Life.

A person I could have met,
someone perhaps in need,
or an altercation deterred,
an idea planted, like a seed.

But now here,
sitting alone,
for only a second until beckoned,
and tossing back and forth ideas.

Talk of a registry,
someone's birthday,
a pizza bought once
and the caffeine quota.

This isn't a waste,
like the fight down 24,
though the direction doesn't matter.
They both suck.

So was the drive back,
but I'll tell you what,
I'm glad I didn't go to spend more money,
instead spending time with people.

That is a need."

# 76 THE AWOKEN

"From fables old,
the story of this hero be told,
of his actions bold,
when he wouldn't fold.

In wars past,
facing impossible odds
against enemies from nightmares.
Bullets the size of your face,

screaming towards you,
to rip you in half.
To steal your life
and break your line.

The line that you made up
to halt the advance of a scourge
that spread across stars and worlds
to extinguish the light of Humanity.

If you took a step back,
you might as well pass your rifle off,
for sooner than a death from the front
a death would step on you from behind.

The world would tremble,
the great cannons far behind
lending their words to the argument.
Artillery on both sides, trading volleys.

But then those rounds would fall on you,
decimating entire companies of Men and Xenos.
The intensity of each explosion rocking your body back,
and beating your morale to the ground.

Armor, tracked and Bipedal,
would roll by your sides,
engaging formations of enemy across the field.
the former bearing direct-fire cannons.

Spitting out their wrath
with a booming cough,
pockets of the enemy suddenly torn apart
at the end of the round trail the tank shot.

The bigger Bipedal beasts,
lumbering slowly to the front.
Each of their step felt by everyone.
A solemn promise of the death they guarantee.

These behemoths, giants made of metal,
bringing to bear rockets, machine guns,
bullets and flame,
their hydraulics screaming as it points its fingers out.

And then there would be you,
the troop.
The individual soldier
in a squad.

Dwarfed by the weapon systems
Humanity threw at the green, hulking Xenos.
Each soldier had almost barely enough
to stand toe-to-toe with the brutes.

One such soldier,
the one they called Marcavius,
a Sergeant of his squad,
was a monster himself.

The one who watched as a young child
in his village during the early times of war,
when Xenos rained down from the skies
and destroyed the life he knew.

These Xenos, standing eight feet tall,
ripped limbs off the men,
tore clothes off the woman,
and did the unthinkable.

He watched them as they cut down his family,
as they obliterated the ground and homes,
as they did unspeakable things to his mother,
and the woman of the village.

The day Marcavius lost his sanity,
and became a survivor of war,
only to become a monster with one purpose:
to destroy those he hated.

The fateful day,
centuries ago, when he rolled out to wage war.
The battle that broke him,
and set him free.

Years had passed since his youth,
twenty since he was seven,
after a few campaigns
a part of the Human Ground Forces.

Now on the ground,
his company in a fierce battle
with the enemy over prime space,
the back of a resource mine.

The battlefield was at the lip of the mine,
a sprawling field with stone and hills,
but much open space that lead to dead Men.
Here, Marcavius waged war.

Starting past the line,
he drew his men forward to suppress the enemy.
The Xenos, themselves armed with large caliber rifles,
brought such weapons to bear.

Afraid, and about to be torn
apart, Marcavius rushed to face them head on,
his squad holding back
to shoot a spray of defiance.

Marcavius, reaching the lead Xenos,
dwarfed by the hulking green monster,
ran underneath the outreached arms
and pulled the trigger after the barrel was placed.

Pure shock hit the enemy,
a Human had never before been so brave,
and they ran toward the lone soldier,
who was working out from under the toppled corpse.

Worse,
the Human line had been pushed back,
and the artillery fire that was raining from above
was retreating as well.

Marcavius had no choice but to fight forward,
or be broken by his own friendly steel rain.
With a mighty strength he was unaware of,
he hefted the enemy's archaic, gigantic gun.

He held a position against the enraged Xenos,
all rushing to crush the soldier,
choosing the claw over the bullet.
Marcavius spun, spraying death to the rushing.

But alas, the magazine went dry,
and he was engulfed.
A moment earlier, surely would have been torn limb from limb.
Had the Biped not moved up the line.

Seeing a group of Xenos,
firing a mighty shoulder cannon into the midst,
all the combatants were killed,
or injured beyond capacitance.

Marcavius,
unmoving,
broken,
destroyed.

The brave soldier was found.
Hero. Picked up and kept alive,
but to a fate that was not public.
An experiment.

Marcavius,
courageous,
glorious,
reborn.

The idea was to keep the warrior alive,
to fight another day.
Though no one knew
that it would be for eternity.

The soldier was subjected
to thousands of operations,
all to practically replace his internals.
All of which were mechanically grafted,

genetically modified,
and painfully installed.
The point wasn't to make a functioning body,
just one that wouldn't age.

The success was horrifying,
the soldier's skin taunt and contorted,
a limb missing,
his skull permanently adorned with a helmet.

An interface,
which finally was plugged in.
The warrior was put to sleep,
and then encased.

The process here was ceremonial,
for Marcavius was the first.
The tomb was filled with life-tech,
and then smelted shut.

The sarcophagus
was then assembled together
to become a fierce,
walking tank.

Standing twenty feet high,
a presence felt in any room.
The beast sat on its haunches.
Ready for war.

Not one person knew what would happen,
when the warrior kept alive inside
was brought to consciousness
to pilot the terrible Juggernaught.

The day had come,
to see if all the resources paid off.
And when all the systems were turned on,
and adrenaline pumped painfully into the entombed solider,

breathing became audible. Suddenly,
the Juggernaught stood up tall,
it's weapons bristling.
Everyone in the corridor held their breath.

Here, the champion of Man,
the soldier twice born.
Now, the owner of a stony voice that commanded.
One that spoke of death and destruction.

One that spoke of pure pain.
One that spoke of a rage, waiting to be wielded.
One that spoke of a bravery never to be exhausted.
This voice, rang out;

<I HAVE AWOKEN.>"

*After writing The Waker, a gentleman emailed me asking me to continue the little sci-fi universe I had the poem set in. So I wrote The Awoken as a backstory for the Juggernaught. It went on from there.*
*The idea was to not only write a fantasy war but also hit some themes I myself mull about in my head. The whole series constitutes not only a make believe war but how some people deal with the real thing, how I myself see it. There will be more tales of the 1st War Machine and its units.*

# 77 CAMPING TRIP

"A memory,
fleeting as it hit me hard,
dropped my jaw slack
as I suddenly remembered its details.

The details that made up the night
we went camping.
Not that I knew what,
or why.

But what I remembered about it,
and the facts that I know this day,
a young man trying to grow up,
it hits hard.

The day?
Not remembered,
for that portion, though maybe not negative,
unfortunately plays no part in this tale.

Stale,
the air of the apartment
as we stumbled into the room,
hands reaching for lights.
Lights that did not come on.

As a child, I think six,
the implications were not immediate.
But I can only imagine
the way my Mother's heart sank.

The Mother of two,
children that caused her so much stress,
gave much more than she ever got,
but sometimes it wasn't enough for life.

Working two jobs,
she barely kept up with payments due,
barely kept her head above water
while feeding two bottomless mouths.

An unpaid bill,
a fault in the line.
I have a feeling it's the former,
a crushing blow to my Mother's pride.

But to us two,
sister and brother,
we looked up at our provider,
our skin cold.

I ran down the hallway, feeling my way through the dark,
not fully understanding the situation,
but jumping in glee as I informed
the two girls the plumbing still worked.

I came back to a few candles lit,
my Sister almost in tears,
my Mother's face stone,
a night ahead full of fears.

The Utah winters were unkind,
the nights were no exception.
Up for interpretation,
the implications of my Mother's next actions.

But before I lay them,
I see now what she did.
Thinking back, and to the person she is,
I am almost brought to cry.

She loved us so much.
Too much. And she made our lives better
than the rough one she had herself
in another place of poverty.

So she exclaims
"Hey! Let's go camping!
Right in the living room!"
And that was all it took!

My sister and I ran to our rooms,
bumping into the doorway in the absence of light,
giggling as we grabbed blankets and pillows.
We never had too much.

But it was enough,
us returning to the couch cushions
being turned into a little fort.
We joined our Mother, the circumstance forgotten.

We sat on blankets and laughed,
forgetting the lack of a hot dinner.
Peanut Butter and Jelly was made,
we were camping, after all!

Stories were spun,
my Mother a master at the craft,
maybe the sole provider
for my racy imagination.

The night crept on,
us cuddling for warmth,
us finally falling asleep,
and then the memory ends.

How rough, that night must have been;
the fact my Mother couldn't provide.
How sad, the crushing feeling
that her children weren't cozy and warm.

But that didn't matter,
because we were camping!
Right in the living room,
having fun.

I guess I always knew I had a little less.
But on this day, the biggest heart in this chest,
I look back at what she did for us,
and all the other stories that can be told.

My Mother, my hero,
made negative into positive,
stress into fun,
a night without electricity,
into a camping trip."

*A memory of my childhood.*

# 78 DOUBT

"Shocking,
the pain is,
grinding my on-rushing train
to a complete and dead stop.

Pain,
in my legs.
Pain,
in my back.

But this isn't the usual
colors of light that dance
all about my body when I am running.
Underneath it all, there's concern.

A reason to stop,
a grit of the teeth
tells me the injury is serious,
or at least more than usual.

I usually brush it off,
blowing off pain for weakness,
but sometimes the knack
for being a real Prince Charming,

the sweet romancing,
the lies that no one's sure
about catch it. This pain,
this is more.

I am stunned,
the realization of what I cannot do
the only thing moving.
For my leg sure isn't.

The kick, useless,
the knee, bends with complaint,
and the fear arises
I may not be able to run!

Or lift,
or longboard,
or surf my life to the left.
I may not be able to function without pain.

And that is painful,
to think all these scenarios through my head
with me being kept back from,
like a dog choking himself on a too-short chain.

Chained,
the fear that's on my heart,
the pain that's on my leg.
I can't believe I hurt myself.

So, dare I say?
Yesterday, I did nothing.
Not one activity, save cook for friends,
and though it hurt to not be running around,

it felt good.
Like a drill,
being pressed too hard into the wood
and the bit no longer biting deeper.

I was pulled back,
blew the dust out the hole,
cleaned the drill bit free from shavings,
and after a minute of enjoyment,

feeling alright,
before going back in
to drill deeper,
smarter, and finish the job.

The drill bit still worn,
my leg still torn,
I hope it heals soon.
I can't stop swimming forward, I'll drown."

# 79 MY SHORTEST POEM

"Isn't.

My proudest moment, barely remembered.

Washed away,
like the hundreds of recruits
who washed out of bootcamp.
Yet I got Company Honorman?

The idea, phenomenal,
but reality makes it irrelevant,
it means nothing now,
save something to be poked fun of.

Like so many other things,
my refusal to bend, my refusal to break,
but my lack of learning from my mistakes,
I suppose I shouldn't be surprised.

You got to own up to the life that you pass,
if you don't, it may be your last
time to consider some people friends.
Many friends,

aren't.
More like people hoarders,
social media changing me into a caricature of who I really am,
this my own fault.

My fantastic life,
isn't. At all,
far from it.
Though, I do indeed enjoy

not putting my discontent out
in the public eye,
for others don't need to see that.
Nor do they want to.

Let the gift of Love,
which I actually DO believe in,
lead my way about town.

Though I wander, I am not lost.
A lie, that isn't.
But other things,
like when I claim I don't feel sad,

can be. Lonely,
I shouldn't feel,
surrounded constantly with friends.
But alone is where I retreat to every night.

Just to wake up to rush
back to the folks who accept my presence,
the vibe that I don't fake,
but make others skeptical.

'Is he really so happy?'
'Is he really so cool?'
'Is he really all these things?'
No.

Well, sometimes.
Let the wave push me down,
let the street lead the way,
let the Sun be chased.

The Sun? Now that I'm sure of.
Let it rise,
come above the hillside.
Let the light come.

'Is the Sun really so bright?'
'Is it really always shining?'
'Is it really so warm?'
Yes,

and I guess I am too.
Well, sometimes.
Just like this short poem. Which,
isn't."

# 80 THE SLEEPLESS

"On this day,
a day like the rest,
the war waged far away,
but not out of reach.

Not for them.
These men, a different breed,
had a passion for lead,
perhaps more than the rest.

Across the horizon,
where battle ravaged both sides,
a convoy rumbled in the foreground.
Six pieces towed,

waiting. Silent,
solemn.
Their presence a slow crawl
to their eventual screams.

Mankind had many weapons,
too many to learn.
One thing that separated Mankind from the Xenos
was the specialization. In turn,

it brought more expertise to the table,
more appreciation, more enthusiasm
to the art that each soldier partook in.
From Infantry,

the squads of brave troops,
armed with little firepower, rifles and grenades were their words.
Versatile to the end.
The wrath of the War Machine at their beck and call.

Along their troop brothers, Heavy Weapons,
and their rapid chatter of death.
High caliber machine gun teams, hand cannons
and shoulder-mounter launchers.

A major asset to the ground forces,
the Air Wing and all its jets,
bombers and gunships,
rain death from above and prowl the skies.

Tanks, treaded,
roll over hills and enemy,
their guns, dreaded,
coughing a fiery end to the Xenos.

The Bipedal armor,
piloted by the very best,
lumbering around and breaking enemy lines,
or holding lines on their own.

The Juggernaught,
ancient warrior of the past,
entombed in their own war machine,
towering over the battle, and winning whole wars.

And then there was Artillery.

That in and of itself was different aspect of war.
Being so far from the battle,
some would say they had it the easiest.
But nothing could be farther from the truth.

They were cannoneers,
artilleryman.
Arty.
The support.

They would pull in,
miles away from the fight,
but still close to danger,
and emplace the six cannons.

Guns, the biggest cannons in the arsenal.
The Cracken Cannon. Its caliber dwarfing
even the mighty weapons of the Bipedals,
or the shoulder cannon of the Juggernaught.

Its operation so conventional it was archaic,
being that the round was loaded into the rear of the cannon,
then the powder charge loaded behind
before the breech closed off the back.

The breech block spins to seal,
sealing off the wrath from the world
before it bursts into manifestation.
The wrath of Humanity.

These artilleryman,
many do not know their struggle.
Their life and death
as they rush to keep up with the battle.

They run up and down the gunline,
spread-loading rounds and powders alike,
to keep the barrage of the guns constant
raining onto the Xenos.

On this day,
a day like the rest,
the Battery is emplaced
with the six guns in sequence.

The order comes down,
and the artillery pieces rear their ugly heads,
giant muzzle brakes looking like mouths of demons,
tongues out, toothless.

Then we men load the piece,
driving two hundred pound rounds into the chamber,
ramming with a hydraulic ram that never worked,
many a loader breaking wrists and fingers when the ram fails.

The round in, the powder pushed behind,
a bag of no less than fifty pounds itself,
ready to propel the round out
with explosion and chemical reaction.

For all the advances passed down,
the war tech made lethal,
the lives extended and convenience evoked,
this way of war was never made anew.

There was no weapon of energy,
just a concept of metal being made
to shoot towards the enemy
with expanding gas. Ancient!

Yet it worked.
The breech closed,
the quadrant set with the tube elevated at the right level,
the deflection ready with the tube on the correct azimuth,

The Battery stands by.
The battle was about to start.
The crew was ready,
a six man group that worked all over the cannon.

The chief, the sergeant of the group,
raised his sword, purely ceremonial.
The First Man readied the lanyard to fire.
The crew plugged their ears.

And so, the last argument of Kings continued,
and Artillery spoke first.
This Battery, part of the 1st War Machine,
7th Regiment. 2nd Battalion. Fira Battery.

Gun 1.
She opens up,
and screams.
And the pillars of the planet shake.

The Battery opens fire,
consuming the air with deafening noise
as all six scream out
hate and discontent.

The rolling wail of the rounds
flying towards their targets
slowly ebbs away
as the crew loads another round.

Thus, the constant roll begins,
thousands of rounds are hefted into place,
loaded, fed powder,
and lit aflame to fly away.

Cannons tubes run hot,
having to be doused with water
to keep the volleys continuous.
Men get tired.

But it is all for the battle so far away.
The fight is now with the man himself,
the will to continue the mission
and keep the cannon speaking.

One gun goes down,
a mechanical failure,
and one man runs forward,
a toolbox in one hand and a pneumatic tank on the other shoulder.

The mechanic, the gun doc,
runs to the downed gun to bring it back into action,
an inherently dangerous job
with such a destructive behemoth.

A Battery's speed
can be defined by how well the Gun Doc is,
and this one has a reputation.
He can fix anything.

So he gets to work,
working in the cradle,
much to everyone's disagreement,
the Gun Doc in the pathway of the cannons recoil.

But fearless is he,
and round and powder in the tube not stopping him,
as he resets the recoil system with oil and gas.
Swift hands make lines and bolts fly about.

Soon the gun is back up,
and joins her sisters
to keeping screaming into the night.
The battle has waged for hours.

Night falls,
and now the men must sleep.
But they cannot.
They will not.

The barrage continues,
much past the limit of the human body,
and the men are falling out
as they load the guns again and again.

To feel the caress of sleep,
to lay down is intoxicating.
But these artillery man cannot stop,
the forces on the frontlines depend on accurate, timely fire.

And so they shoot,
and some of the men keel over.
Dying from exhaustion,
the most sad and common fate of these artillerymen.

These sleepless men,
unable to rest due to the mission,
and even if they could lay down,
sleep would be arrested by the concussion.

The battle wages on,
the rounds wail off.
The Guns speak,
the men get no sleep.

The Xenos die."

# 81 THREE THOUSAND THIRTY

"The buildings,
they were massive, once.
Once, you could see them from a distance,
they would peek their spires up as you approached.

But these buildings toppled down,
to make way for the intrusive patron.
The new patron who pushed the citizens out,
and into the land around.

Such abandonment was distasteful,
bringing much hatred for the Forest,
but here we are, living in little swathes of concrete,
small Cities all that remained.

The Trees, they came,
turning our Cities into Forests.
They came and tore our skyscrapers,
those which used to shine so beautiful.

And now?
Instead of the streets, choked with cars,
instead of the air full of toxins and pollutants,
instead of people milling about with no appreciation of the streets,

there are Forests. Forests!
Just these Trees, all around,
with pathways and sprawling branches.
All sorts of trees and woods.

From redwood to cedar,
evergreen and maple,
cottonwood and birch,
oak and mahogany.

These Trees! They just stand there,
providing cover for the floor,
giving a cover to the creatures that make it their home.
When it rains, it makes music.

These Trees, they just provide air,
making the life-giving breath pure,
giving to us land a color green
that sparkles in the morning.

Can you believe it?
We lost all the biggest Cities,
all the monuments of Man's conquisition,
all the concrete plains.

Fabled places called York,
Sadle, Daygo and Frisco.
Orlins and Angels. Boss-tone,
Shishcoggo and Fillie.

The natural way of life
gave way to the Trees that came,
and we stood helpless
as the Forests tore into our homes.

Made us homeless,
for now many people live in the Forests now,
making due with the sad existence of being in nature
constantly. A travesty.

So sad, this intrusive manner
the land changed ownership.
For the Cities had been here first,
right?"

# 82 EXTRA ENERGY

"Another!
I need another,
please, if you will,
I'd like to drink one more.

Oh, goodness,
I love the feeling.
I mean, it's not too apparent.
Well, actually. Is it?

I don't feel a physical difference,
as in my skin crawling, or itching,
though I kind of feel my heart beat.
Like it's dancing!

I want to get down tonight,
maybe do a little dance,
make a little bit of love.
The usual.

The supplier of so much energy,
gee, I'm not too sure what is the cause,
except that I can't help but want more.
It's not like the restlessness I get when I sleep in too late,

or the second I get from being up too late.
Nor the energy I get when I'm heated,
trying to lift just ten more pounds on the barbell.
I love that energy.

Nay, this is one fueled by the bean,
first crack, I believe,
for the roast isn't too dark.
Oh my goodness,

the energy felt right now,
can you feel it?
Thank goodness it's Saturday,
I think I just got paid?

No matter, I want to party the day away,
or night. Not sure,
but if I have enough caffeine,
I'll last the whole time!

The energy feels good,
like the end of the night when I finally crash,
though I enjoy the burn.
Burn, baby, burn, like an inferno,

let me ask you a question.
Want to be my lover?
I'll make you feel like no other,
but another might argue against that.

Whatever,
just give me another coffee,
I've definitely had too much,
and that's just fine.

This is the night,
where everything will feel alright,
well. Maybe.
As long as I keep drinking the Joe.

And now I'm tired.
All over the place,
like this piece.
But not a space put to waste.

I'll ride this energy out,
for I always have enough.
I might run out eventually,
but not any time soon.

I have an espresso in front of me,
well, had.
Maybe I'm an addict?
No. Just a advocate!"

# 83 NORTHWEST SON

"Grey,
matching the concrete beneath my feet,
the skies seems to always be,
and I love it.

The smell of this place
is a mix that I love,
like the taste of a piroshky
made with salmon dip.

The walk of this particular lady,
an early riser like me,
the metro full of people like me,
moving about their day, whatever that means.

Many walks taken,
more it seems that were wet,
being rained on,
but in a loving way.

The raindrops wouldn't ever be harsh,
more like a caress,
keeping me company even on the lonely sidewalk,
smothered in rhymes.

A young boy,
standing on the corner,
waiting at the bus stop beat-boxin,
his life altered by what was in his Walkman.

Planets that were Dug,
a Quest called Tribe,
a Clan of Wu
and Illmatic filled my ears,

while the Northwest filled my lungs,
the grey, gold and the green,
with weather unable to plan for,
it's colder than it seems.

The sun was even out,
yet a jacket was always on,
there was no in-between.
The only one was me,

going from Westlake to Downtown,
University and Southcenter,
Stadiums and Kent,
sitting in the back with half-broken headphones.

Joe-Metropolitan, that was me,
sitting sideways with my town-mates,
a transfer in my hand,
hopping off at 1st Ave,

walking up Pike to get some eats,
chinese cuisine well done,
passing old Filipino men
speaking in their native tongue.

Lost in deep thought,
as much as a fifteen year old can be,
saving my breath,
the way my heart beat in my chest.

Life wasn't easy,
many bus times missed,
but I was quite happy in the City,
this one only remembered.

The rain that always came,
the people who were always around,
the smiles and bright green
pouring out for the Sounders

and Hawks, though the latter
only seems to be recently.
Either way,
the love of this place

was felt as I walked around the streets,
generally alone,
just a wandering youth
finding shops,

places to eat or take someone to see,
seeing the sights as well as scoffing tourists,
laughing at the walls and art
that made this place unique.

The love for the place and its grey skies,
its Metro system and rain,
coffee and constant construction,
Puget Sound sounds and smells,

brings me back to my youth.
It isn't my longing,
it isn't where I want to call my own.
But it is indeed my first home.

So busy claiming the Sun,
giving way to the beach and surf
and Ocean and waves and the
Golden State of mind

I forget my own roots,
my Evergreen State. Not that I hid this one,
but the fact of the matter is,
I'm a Northwest Son."

*I like to think I will end up in California, will most likely end up in California, and I love California, but I can't forget where I came from. Washington is where my Mother is, my family, my home I was raised in.*

*I want to end in the bottom of the West Coast, but I started from the top of it.*

# 84 THE DREAMERS

"Even from the beginning of training,
it always felt like a dream.
Because you were always locked in,
never exposed to the world.

That being the case,
encased like a stone,
the driver of any tank was subjected
to a dream-like state.

The days of training
in cockpits, an exact replica,
hopping in for hours at a time
into the seat,

only to watch all the light disappear
with the hatch closing shut.
Then to feel around the dark
until you found the switch to start the simulation.

The buttons, switches,
handle and levers would blip alive with a blue hue
as the screen would illuminate.
And then you would see around you.

In training, it was all made up,
like any dream. But there you were,
piloting a tank around the battlefield,
feeling the hydraulics rock you

as the cannons above your head
coughed again and again.
Simulation of course.
Different sensations were experienced.

The single, accurate cannon
of the Shock Tank,
designed to punch through fast and hard,
would destroy any light Xenos enemy.

The Shock was a fast, maneuverable beast,
comparatively. Rushing around the lines of infantry
on the screen, you could fly about,
the turret bearing quickly to fire off its load.

The same simulator would give you the sensation
of piloting a tank of fire,
an effective killer of the Xenos scourge,
a definitive end to the hulking enemy.

Aptly named, a danger to all,
the Blaze tank was slower to handle,
meant to mop up the aftermath of a push
rather than punch through and lead.

The turret, with its nozzle instead of cannon,
spewed out flame in a wash of heat,
lighting those unfortunate to be in its path
in a sticky, painful inferno.

With a small range,
however, it was forced to push closer.
The clank of the tread that gave a solemn note
to the fiery end to come

also lowered the Blaze Tank's chance of survival.
Armored heavier than the Shock for this purpose,
though still susceptible to being overwhelmed,
the salamander had a tendency to exploding in a great fireball.

But all of that knowledge is lost,
as the pilot drives the tank around.
His only window a screen,
a picture painted inches from his eyes.

Composed of hundreds of small vid feeds,
as to eliminate the possibility
of going blind in a battle.
Sure, the rumble of the engine

toiling away at churning the treads
was felt in the seat. The rock
and concussion of the cannons felt.
Even the feeling of an eighty ton tank moving.

But it was all just a dream.
You would begin to lose the reality of it all.
Time would melt together,
piloting this machine

until you didn't feel it all.
Just a floating sense,
just like in a dream.
At least, in training.

An exception was the Wardog.
A tank toeing the line of impracticality.
A bully on the battlefield.
The pride of any Tank Regiment.

Learning the Wardog took a different simulator,
the incredibly cramped cockpit again
shutting you off from the world.
A slow boot up.

This light was green,
a hue that helped with the smoke and fog
of a battle waging on.
A machine so large,

yet destructive. Crewed by six,
two more than needed for the other tanks,
two cannons thorned out of the wide turret,
twin arms that cocked back and forth.

Two men per cannon,
rocking the pilot cockpit fiercely
whenever it blasted. These cannons
boasted more size than those of the Bipedals.

Only trumped by the Cracken cannons
of the Artillery Regiments,
the Wardog wandered the field slowly,
and declared its ownership of life

as it dealt death.
Cannons shooting one at a time,
driving a pilot to nosebleeds
and migraines.

These dreams would blur together,
until you went to battle.
The first real battle,
where you crawled your way into an actual tank.

Given a unit, 1st War Machine.
2nd Regiment Tanks.
1st Battalion.
Beta Company.

We climbed into the Wardog,
a larger-than-life machine,
it's double wide chassis
crowned with a double wide turret.

The cannons bearing menacingly,
as we circled around the treads to the side
to the access hatch on the rear.
Sliding through the small space,

four men prepping the cannons,
passing a fifth Tank commander,
finally dropping into the pilot seat,
I closed the hatch.

Complete darkness,
time to start this dream.
I felt for the switch,
and ignited the Wardog.

The dream blurs again,
but this time on my green screen,
I see objects moving about,
watching them be split apart by rounds of my cannon.

My dream blurs,
watching infantry be ripped to shreds by Xenos.
Figuratively, by the enemy's tactics.
Literally, by the enemy's claws.

My dream blurs,
watching a Blaze Tank burst into flames,
humans trying to crawl out
before being picked up and pulled into halves.

The four Wardogs of Beta Company
roll through, decimating.
I watched this dream unfold and I lost sensation.
I was in the middle of the battle,

but now I couldn't feel the tank.
I couldn't feel the treads, the cannons,
the rumble or anything.
I was floating,

and I was nowhere in the battle.
Just an observer,
slighting moving my hands
and watching my screen change perspective.

Even the orders from the Tank commander
weren't consciously heard,
but they were followed somehow,
this dream turning more surreal.

I lost a sense of reality.
I no longer knew what was a simulation,
what was real,
what was danger or imagination.

The cannons concussion had turned our brains to mush
or maybe that's the excuse I made.
I had lost my mind.
I was just dreaming.

Was the battle over?
Was I in a different one?
Was this a different campaign?
Whoa, is that a Juggernaught in the distance?

No, I'm just dreaming.
Someone please help me,
it dawned on me as I woke up.
Not in my cot on the Warship,

but in the cockpit.
A dream,
turned into a reality.
It was still my first battle."

*Sometimes a war is not fought on the battlefield, but in the mind.*

# 85 EXIT

"I only have an hour and a half,
but I decline the invitation
to laugh at myself,
the inclination of being content.

Content with what?
Just leaving at the moment,
that's all. Not a comment
on myself, for I like myself.

Quite content with myself,
but still working on that too.
Like my figure and manners,
Excuse me, yes, how are you?

I'm not trying to leave,
but I should, I start my next shift soon,
I still need to eat, shave my face,
I can't stand the scruff look.

I look like a buffoon, and perhaps
others do too,
but my opinion isn't too important
at the moment. I need to exit,

to egress, to skate back
to my car and drive back
to my apartment to come right back
to town.

Back and forth,
I definitely don't mind,
but I'm sort of jaded
with the fact the day is almost already gone.

It's not, it's still in front of me,
but I hardly know myself
if we know nobody else,
and what I know is,

I need to exit.
I need to stop what I'm doing,
as others say to me,
and move on out.

But I don't,
or won't. Pick one,
as I finally pack up the laptop,
gathering my thoughts

near the edge of the day.
Phone going off,
but I ignore the notification,
it's a distraction to the day around me.

So many people,
girls in sundresses, walking delicately
in high heels that always catch my eye,
escorted by gentleman in ties,

floral patterns galore,
flowing hair and trimmed beards.
They trump the presence of the regulars.
That's always how the weekends are.

And now the weekends gone.
Time to exit,
like the Sun setting his tireless body.
Time to exit."

# 86 A REFLECTION

"Imagine, for a second,
the excitement the lad had,
when he first came across a pond,
and saw his one reflection.

To see his own smile,
brush his slight hair off his brow,
give a wink and pass,
thoughts lifted.

But better than a reflection
off the pond that is so easily distorted,
a polished mirror serves better,
giving to light all details.

The drawback? Just that,
seeing all details and imperfections.
Scrutiny is the enemy,
detracting from the imagery.

But! Better still,
than the mirror on the wall,
is the eyes of blue
you have that calls.

To see yourself in another,
is the best reflection of all,
for all you see is the good,
the gold that makes people fall.

But you,
you get it,
the power of word,
and like me, you use it,

even more fluid than I.
Provoked by each other
to enjoy each other's works,
another sword master in my presence.

We may even trade blows!
How exciting, the image,
two poets dueling out,
ink spilling over the field of white.

Artists are everywhere,
everyone is deep.
But most never dive,
and you? You went in steep,

the fall you float down
with your words are glorious,
I look forward to reading more.
And perhaps, soon,

seeing those eyes of blue."

# 87 THE STARTER

"And so it begins,
my own little journey.
And to who but I,
shall it be made known,
that I rush to see it to the end?

The one who loves said words,
would be a good start.
But, she is foolish, to be sure;
as for that was why we fell apart.

The one who loves gold,
who values the material,
would never understand the momentous value
of the invaluable value
of a valueless rhyme.

Victory! I cry,
for I march on,
and the weapon unsheathes,
and blood is soon spilled.

My swordplay littering the field.
Of it, comes the spray,
and like art, it paints a picture,
one as bright and sure as day.

To who shall it be made known,
that I swing my blade!
Deftly hands swish the air
and I can finally escape.

The blade falls, the blood bled,
and my artwork becomes apparent.
My swordplay, well-practiced,
comes like a Masters works hint.

And to the one who shall read
these words on these pages,
it is YOU that it shall be known,
that is made to be made known,

my own little struggle,
my own little journey.
Poetry is my art,
the pen my blade,
its ink its blood.

It is the shadow of a man,
the light of the soul.
The window to the mind,
just take hold of the door.

Release your mind, as I have done,
and dive into this book.
See what I see, paint the image,
and you will soon be took,

to the trail I walk,
my own little journey.
As I was set on it, come now,
Because of you, I hurry.
To write again! About my little journey"

# 88 AFTERNOON TUNE

"The trumpets let up,
softly. So softly. Just how,
exactly, can a man begin to describe
the sound that they give.

Even more so. They speak
to a man's soul. The pure,
raw emotion they evoke.
Even better, emotion put into the sound.

So here I lay, letting the smoky lounge
enter my head. The smell of whiskey,
cigarette smoke, and perfume assault me.
They paint the stage for the tune.

The woman now speaks, the trumpet silent,
and she sings just to me.
Of our first dance, our first kiss,
it doesn't matter.
It's just to me.

The other teething prohibitioners
circle the stage, and she coos.
But they laugh and drink,
and never grasp the longevity of the tune.

And I turn, nudging my glass aside,
slamming the scotch down; it burns.
My eyes water, not from the liquor,
I just can't escape the song,
the trumpet speaks to me.

My lover approaches, but like me,
she is entranced by the slow gaunt of the tune.
She may see the stage different, for she,
unlike me, is in reality.

I am not. I am lost at sea,
though no Ocean is near. I speak of
my mind. I am not here, in this bed.
I am at this bar, slugging away at this bottle.

I am there, the music live,
the piano dancing its tune into the room.
The ladies walk by, the men blow smoke,
and I am entranced by the stage,
the band and its slow dance.

The grace, it plays, and goes down smooth,
like an old warm finger,
and warms my soul, like said shot
warms my belly.

I drink, and listen, and fall back in love
with the tune that plays.

I snap to reality, and push next on the phone.
The room gone, the smoke dissipated,
The jazz over. I switch to the next
Pandora station."

# 89 NON-PROFIT

"I walk down the alley,
pushing through the large crowd,
minglers, sipping on this
or that, trying to decompress.

Impressed, a larger crowd than expected,
or more so than a normal Wednesday night,
but you can't combat too much
the day picked for event to set flight.

Here, for beer,
the draft, to be specific,
a dollar of the purchase donated
to a local charity. The real reason

I had showed my face. Though
I'm not an unwelcome sight,
I guess I don't have whole crowds moving
like a star walking on stage of his show.

Let's make them,
home is where the heart is,
back to where we started,
and my heart is all over tonight,

as I walk all over,
pointing, asking, what beer they want,
racking up the bill and passing back and forth
between bars and tables like I bussed drinks.

And I did,
all purchased by me,
a man sober,
making a walk from table with glasses full,

pats on the back as I slid by,
all-of-a-sudden a popular guy,
buying everyone in the pub a beer,
the bartender, a friend,

giving me grief as I bought my twentieth drink;
'Why you doing this?'
I smiled and was handed another glass
as I walked outside to hand off the amber bliss.

A question often asked,
Why you do that?
How you doing it with smile?
What is this guy on?

I call it my way of life,
it's no problem except the fact
that maybe I don't care,
it's no fair

to some that I'm happier with less.
Too late, in walks a pretty face,
the original person who had invited
me here in the first place.

She worked at a Non-profit,
who was working with the charity,
and was ecstatic as ever
when she walked up to me.

We sat and talked,
mostly about the lack of participation,
though with some bought beer,
I guess I made a sizable dent.

She smiled and was almost in tears,
asking me 'Why I did this?'
I smile and reply with a wink in my eye,
a little bit of this,

a little bit of that.
A whole lot of nothing
that keeps me on track.
I keep it cool.

Calm helps too.
I just like giving,
and helping,
I don't want anything in return.

We sat in the dark pub,
people chattering away to our left,
us two sitting across from each other,
passing subjects with smiles and agreements,

lack of sleep,
dedication to work,
lack of relationships,
longing for love and all things considered,

I feign to leave and pay my tab,
a substantial amount more than it usually is,
and come back to tell her
my secret.

It's nothing.
Happiness is a choice,
and I keep it cool,
I stay calm.

I'm just trying to stay grounded.
I'm always high,
so high,
off love and conversation."

# 90 THE RESTED

"Only the best had the right to prowl.
The very best. Minds exalted.
Bodies, monuments to physical perfection.
Soul, zealous.

The dedicated,
edge of fanatics.
The best recruits of Basic Course,
going through the training like all do,

get swooped away from the rest
at an earlier stage than the other soldiers,
who get split up to their perspective specialties
at the very end of four long months.

Instead,
after two months the top are picked out,
one night they are in the rack,
the next disappearing from the morning roll call.

No questions asked from the instructors,
recruits fearing for their lives as three or four
of their own suddenly vanished,
unaware they escaped a fate deemed terrible,

but only by those who undertook it.
The path followed one of thorns,
pain and blood that was hidden
by the shining armor worn bright.

The Knights of the War Machine.
The ones who earn the right to prowl.
The ones who adorn the suits of armor,
the Bipedals of the 6th Regiment.

The Bipedals,
hulking monsters standing even taller than the Xenos,
bested only by the Juggernaught himself.
The ones who prowl.

But before one can even try,
the awful process that grinds men to dust
and monsters into the ranks
starts behind a curtain.

In order to pilot a Bipedal,
the link of man and machine must be bridged.
The time it took to send a brain signal
to the hand was too long.

When it came to milliseconds,
it mattered,
especially in the battlefield,
wielding the armament of Princes and Kings.

The secretly taken recruits,
unfortunately unaware to their fate,
are asked to sleep.
And sleep they would.

They sleep,
to awaken to their bodies being shredded.
Muscle and sinew cut,
bones cracked,

the process to prowl
a necessary evil,
in order to withstand the suit that envelops these men.
The Bipedal is unforgiving.

The skeleton elongated,
to make these men stand seven feet tall.
The spine and brain interfaced
to spill neurons onto a relay.

The process left everyone scared,
but still human.
These suits were made to be taken on and off,
the pilot was still a man after battle.

They would be asked to sleep,
the surgically altered pilots,
and sleep they would
secretly. In the depths of the War Ship,

never to be seen once by the rest of the warriors,
aside from the caretakers who commit to a Band of Bipedals.
Depending on the suit,
a Band of brothers was formed.

The process,
leaving the tall, muscle bound,
rebuilt men,
slightly closer to machine than not.

Slightly altered from their race.
Slightly insane, but not from war.
But zealous dedication. They are less human,
but more Man than their fellow soldiers.

They are indoctrinated,
after surviving their surgeries,
to remain loyal to the cause of Man,
to have an undying fervor to kill the Xenos.

The psychotic warriors,
prowling into whole companies of enemy
just to further the mission of Humankind,
and destroy the scourge that was destroying us.

All men, all fighters in a War Machine,
shared a common interest to defeat the Xenos,
but the Bipedal pilots truly had an Ethos,
they lived and breathed the death of the enemy.

Being brainwashed,
altered,
they finally learn their suit,
the ferocious walkers that prowl.

The Band of brothers' number so small,
six pilots per,
one for their six Prince Bipedals.
A Xenos problem,

with hands that maneuvered deftly,
the ten foot bipedal pushed past lines
so as to close the distance of its machine gun palms,
each spreading the hatred the pilot had.

The Prince could even jog,
an experienced pilot bringing the suit to crush through,
stomping troops and then opening up its hands,
spinning and foiling combat formations.

The shoulder cannon it had on the right,
like a wicked lance that stuck up,
could be dropped down and lined up,
punching through Xenos armor and heavies,

should the Prince need a bigger punch.
Sharing the cannon of a Shock Tank,
the pilot who bore the Bipedal
was indeed a prowler of the battle.

But all Princes bow to the King,
the destructive, wider killer.
Piloted alongside the Prince,
these were magnificent to watch.

Instead of two hands that spewed lead,
the machine guns were traded for a semi-auto,
two-hundred round cannons.
The awkward length of these

spilt out past the elbows,
like each arm had a too long a forearm
that grew past both the front and back,
fingers still on the end of the cannon.

The King,
after decimating the enemy from afar,
after running dry of its rounds,
would move up to face the enemy head on.

Having no other weapons saved the elbow cannons,
now used air pressure to slay,
the back of the chamber pistons
punching holes with hydraulics.

The King
would grab onto the Xenos,
while its elbows cocked back and fired,
firing through the hand,
and whatever grasped in its palm.

The enemy would bow, indeed,
the pilots feeling invincible
as it wade through and grabbed onto running scourge,
blowing through its fingers chunks of green.

The privileged prowlers,
surviving the pain,
the surgeries,
the indoctrination.

One man crews running around the field,
Princes and Kings waging war.
Until joined by the outcast.
The Abominations.

Affectionately referred to as 'Boms,
the twelve foot monsters,
piloted by two monsters,
to kill monsters.

A monster lost in translation,
bristling with weapons,
left hand armed with a machine gun
and a wrist flamer in likeness of the Blaze turret,

and the cannon hand of the King
adorning the right arm
and a rocket pod on the shoulder above,
'Boms brought battles to a close.

The Bipedals, Bands of suits,
rushing into battles
to fight. Almost,
as if, to find release.

To any soldier on the field,
any Tank crew,
and even to the Cracken cannons of the Artillery Regiment.
The Bipedals were gods.

But unbeknownst to their fellow men,
did the pilots want death.
Their life, a constant battle.
The side-effects of the implanted interface.

A reason prominent
in their secluded existence,
the pilots did indeed go mad,
from the constant pain their brain endured.

A reason prominent
in their indoctrination,
to pledge their life to mankind,
for the secret of their painful existence wasn't a surprise.

Only to the pilots was the life
ahead a complete surprise,
the horrible fate befalling them
turning them into hunters.

Prowlers.
Their only release, death.
One of combat,
the zealous Bipedal pilots,

charge into battle not to win,
not to inspire,
not to lead,
but die.

To be awarded that succulent sleep,
ever alluding to the fact
only true sleep
will eliminate the raging headaches,

the crushing buzzing,
and the constant itching that raked their whole bodies
as soon as they were pulled from the suits.
The only relief sleep.

And sleep they did.
But the next campaign would come,
the pulsing red light ebbing with the alarm
that would evoke them from their slumber.

Their beds comfortable,
their rooms spacious,
their awakening met immediately
with a horrible existence.

These privileged pilots
sleep as much as they can.
These men,
rested, detest being awoken.

Rush, the pilots do,
zealous to the end,
to run into their suits,
start the Bipedals,

the engines blasting on,
burning hot as the legs churn
and rush forward.
The launch

off the Warship,
under a Magpad,
over the battle lines.
And then touch down.

The secret existence of the pilots,
the lies of their zeal,
make their search of release
all the more real.

They run to die,
they prowl.
They search for true sleep.
And they rarely ever get it.

The Bipedals were made so well.
The pilots so brainwashed.
The pain almost unbearable.
A conspiracy?

No. A master plan.
An inhumane plan.
A plan so wrong,
it worked."

*Special forces has always been so awe inspiring to me. But I can't imagine what it would be like to be one. Sure, if I put my entire being into it I may have had a chance to discover it for myself, but as an Artillery Mechanic it just seemed impossible and, eventually, unappealing.*
*Don't misunderstand, I obviously have the utmost respect for all Recon, MARSOC, Special Forces Marines and all special forces in general. This poem is an attempt at writing a piece on the elite of my own little sci-fi world going off my own insight of the military and our own elite.*

# 91 THE PHONE CALL

"The phone chirps,
loud and obnoxious,
interrupting my train of thought
as I spin my latest poem.

Piqued, I answer,
my monotone voice
stony as it recites
my unit and title.

The answer is a fellow Marine,
one from a station north,
his sole job
to pursue a few good young men.

The job, this time, however,
is to alert.
As he explains one of my own is in danger
I drop everything.

The scene halting,
people looking at me as I demand more information,
this time from my own phone,
barking orders and surprising patrons.

I'm already out the door,
paying the tab before I even answer
why I'm yelling into my phone,
relaying information up and down the chain.

I bomb the hill,
my longboarding wobbling dangerously
from the speed, my bag on my shoulder,
my phone in my ear,

finding the Marine in need,
his voice blubbering from the speaker.
No matter what happened,
for I had no clue anyway,

I had to get to there.
My higher already on his way,
the prevention of something foolish
my sole mission.

Driving, now,
speeding past people and cars
as I zip up the highway to the station,
and find the Marine against the wall,

sitting on his duff.
Relief.
I walk up and take the situation,
the matter being suppressed.

Moving in to comfort,
putting everyone inside in chairs,
higher ranked Marines and the Navy Corpsman
arrive to resolve the issue.

The young Lance Corporal scorned,
a girl who did him wrong,
as rough as it is,
we reason he needs to be tough.

The Marine, calmer,
starts to fall at ease
as we are there for our brother.
I don't want to imagine

if I hadn't taken that call seriously.
Or if I had not paid attention
to the phone call barely heard.
A blur of events.

No idea if he had picked suicide,
but the youth had broken down. His fate?
We are always there for our brethren,
poetry can wait."

## 92 A WOMAN FORGOTTEN

"I love her.
I would be lying if I said I didn't.
I knew it,
from the day she kissed my lips.

That first time,
where my soul was so young,
and hers so wise.
She healed my heart.

I love everything about her.
The good and the bad.
All days, considering there's
no bad days.

Not with her,
everyone had me smiling,
longing to be in her,
and to never leave her side.

It's been weird,
being away from her.
There are so many others,
many close and interesting.

But nothing comes close to her,
the Coast that she resides
and even the part she sleeps
calls to me as my rightful home.

Nothing comes to her skin,
the way it feels against mine.
But I barely remember,
time washing away the memories we shared

like a tide coming in,
each swell crashing onto the shore,
and wiping clean the beach of moments;
her and I the co-stars.

But I listen to songs that remind me of her every day,
I write poetry about her without her knowing,
I catch myself looking at pictures of us united.
I love her so much.

I don't want to forget her,
she's the love of my life.
She made my life better,
she gave me something to strive for.

The eventual road,
the trip to her place,
the preparation of my car
to speed into her arms.

I would run,
clothes flailing off,
shoes tumbling aside
as I pushed us into her room,

and she let me ride her,
if I made the effort to paddle out.
The only time my mind's most clear,
is when she's near.

I remember her,
the sounds she made,
the feelings she gave me,
with the melding of mind, body, and soul.

I can't express it enough,
how being lost at sea,
she found me,
and swept me ashore

to an island of sanity.
Positivity, happiness.
This lady,
both night and day,

kept me afloat
while I sat on my board,
my giant buster blade,
my wave weapon she allowed.

I haven't forgotten.
I remember her caress,
her smells.
Her loving ebb.

The crash of the crest,
the souls she saves,
the life she gives
with each sacred wave."

# 93 NOTICE

"Looking out the window,
a fine placed window over the sink,
it was nice to watch the sunlight
dance all over the suds of dishwashing soap.

The small kitchen behind me,
a small table and a single chair,
lit with only the morning light,
slowly brightened as the clouds moved.

The small stove besides me,
it's little flame making an egg cackle
as it turned edible,
fit so nicely with its decor.

The loose, lazily laid tiling
was peeling due to age
and a lack of quality.
Or perhaps proper care.

The steel, thin chair
that sat in front of my eating place
had no cushion to assist
the cold reality of a lonely, small apartment.

The egg finished,
picked up and slid onto a saucer
along with toast made
with a wire coat hanger, bent into a rack

that held said bread
over an open flame.
Though from experience,
you had to watch it or it would smoke,

and then you'd done it.
The pesky fire alarm,
I'm certain mischievously placed in the kitchenette ceiling,
would advertise my poor cooking skills.

On the radio set by the window,
my beautiful, lovely lady
Bessie would wail away,
telling me how nobody knows her

when she's down and out.
Shoot, let me tell you,
Ms. Smith,
when you're down and out,

not one penny,
and all my so-called friends
are out having a ball.
I've never felt so low,

the classifieds full of jokes
and weak jobs
that I can't seem to ever find unfilled.
Boot-leg liquor bottle

washing down the egg
and burnt toast.
No place to go,
face shaved with sink water,

the pillow, sheets and bed put away
to make the couch a couch,
the dark apartment came alive
with the opening of the door.

The city sounds filling the room,
car horns buzzing and paperboys hollering,
the busy bussing of men and woman
making a living

sounded so unappetizing.
Well, here I go,
as I place my Flat Cap on my parted hair,
I begin to lock the door behind me,

and notice the Eviction Notice
pinned to the door
underneath the 760
I resided in. Funny,

I lived on the first floor,
yet had a 700 steed.
Or is it stead? Instead, the notice is read.
Down and out, indeed."

# 94 THE DEATH BREATHERS

"Aliens, they are.
Extraterrestrials.
They are insane,
these people.

They walk around their planet,
trying to claim happiness,
yet they're so far from it,
it's a sad fact in itself.

The idea of breathing
the one thing that kills us?
Inconceivable!
Disgusting!

People, strange people
fly about all over their world,
and suck in the air that's poison,
breathing in long and deep.

Every. Single. Day. Toxic!
Don't they know what they're inhaling?
Why would you do that to yourself?
Why would you commit yourself to death?

Maybe it was a species-wide fetish,
a slow death they all partake,
from the moment they are born,
and their very first breath,

to the last breath drawn,
finally sealing their fate.
Like a mass commitment to a life
no longer than a century.

We could all live forever,
our cells never fall apart,
as would theirs,
had they finished changing their atmosphere.

Yet,
they are now fanatics,
committed to keeping the air poisonous,
to keep the small amount of purities from growing.

Time is the champion,
and we're all the challengers,
yet they handicap themselves
in the fight of life.

By breathing in oxygen,
the breath of death,
these people of Earth,
Mankind, leave nothing left."

# 95 THIS WAY TOO

"Hesitation,
a strong hand,
kept mine from typing.
From pushing the send button.

Be patient,
I told myself.
She's coming.
She'll come.

No, she's not,
the fact of the matter is
she isn't wanting to be
with the likes of me.

Goodness, just chill,
my stomach calm from an earlier dish,
she said she'd meet me at 8.
Ish.

Don't text her,
just write a poem.
Ok, is that her?
NO. Calm.

I laugh out loud,
sitting here waiting for you,
the wooden boards
gritty with the countless steps taken on it.

Now housing a poet,
waiting for another.
And from stage right,
or at least my right,

she walks past the alleyway,
peering into it,
catching my glance,
and lets a smile emerge.

As does one on my own face,
your outfit cute,
your face, beaming.
We embrace, warm.

Walked into the Alibi,
a story that we could always use,
we've been here the whole time.
Right?

Right into colloquy,
low voices and high gravity,
alcohol content steep,
subjects deep.

I get high off intelligent conversations,
and you're no exception,
if anything,
you're quality bud;

a quality drug
of positivity.
A personality
that happens to be intoxicating.

We talk, I stare,
your eyes like pools of blue,
deep and cool,
inviting and coy.

We enjoy each other,
slight touches and fingertips wander,
you finally lean,
we decompress.

Talking about music, look
at the art on the wall, chalk,
the poem we just wrote, talk
about out passions.

The night winds down,
it's time for you to exit.
But I follow you this time,
and we walk hand in hand.

Bid our goodbyes,
a slow embrace
turns into arms around waist by me,
arms around my neck by you.

Towards you, I lean,
with a slight denial. I stop,
but then to my surprise,
a sparkle in your gorgeous blue eyes,

your lips find themselves against mine.
A kiss not long,
but sweet,
and I definitely want to participate in more.

Maybe sometime soon,
or later on. Either way,
I just want to say...
I'm falling for you.

Hoping that you feel this way, too."

# 96 THE DROWSY

"What can you do,
what do you do,
in a situation like this.
Insinuation,

if you could call it that,
that the idea of fighting
with next to nothing
was a good one

was hard pressed in our minds.
But you know better
than to assume the higher ups
had your best interest in mind.

Mine? To stay alive,
the last of the original squad.
Before it became awash
with new blood,

eager soldiers,
unaware of the monsters that awaited them.
Their young and eager minds
full of propaganda and hate.

Their fresh love
for the aspect of war
still a twinkle in the eye
I barely remember having.

But that was all before my first campaign.
Like them,
green to the idea of war,
I was part of the rest.

Training, the four months
that grinded all of us
to dust, like ashes
blown in the air

from the tragedy of a volcano
erupting onto the town below.
Ashes, the aftermath of a furnace
incinerating its doomed content.

I soon became so sleepy,
the countless hours awake
paving the way to my eternal drowse.
I could never seem to correct my photoperiod.

But what was lacking
was the end of Basic Course.
The shock of a few recruits 'dropping out'
after only two months. The very best of our company,

never to be seen or heard of again.
There were whispers they had been
treasonous, though who knows of their fate.
It was only ten or so.

But after the whole ordeal,
the wish of my dream to pilot the King,
or Prince, or even an Abomination,
was washed away.

I wanted to prowl,
to stroll in any Bipedal,
but it wasn't to be.
The choice wasn't up to me,

just the observation
of the data collected on me
during the four months of hardship.
It lead me away.

Away from the Airwing,
the flying fighters of the War Machine.
The idea of strafing the surge of Xenos
was to stay grounded.

The hope of sitting in the back of the line,
in what must be an easy life,
the larger men of Artillery
I wouldn't call my brethren.

The crewman of Shock Tanks,
especially the drivers,
always seemed to be in some daze.
Not assigned to me, however.

Nay. I was sent to another
conspiracy. Here, instead,
I would not be clad in steel,
not armed with cannons,

not given wings to fly.
Instead,
a single rifle,
and some grenades.

Disappointment was in all our faces,
for no one wanted to be Infantry.
Fodder.
Dead meat.

Men to be sent to the Xenos
to be slaughtered.
Mindless formations of men
that would litter the battlefield.

We seemed to only get in the way
or Armor and Bipedal.
When we first formed up,
our ranks rid of the recruits

that had spent four months
living their lives with us 'leftovers',
We stood in pockmarked formation,
and made tighter ranks when ordered.

Then a man came out. A MAN.
A man who was a Man.
He stood like a statue,
shoulders broad and back, as though pinned.

He was no giant,
but he was enormous.
Not his size,
but his stature.

This was a Man who had survived Xenos.
This was a Man who had seen his men die,
seen his men kill,
this was a Man who had killed.

The Man was our commanding officer.
He spoke fire,
and it lit us aflame.
He told us to stop.

To stop being weak. To not need sleep,
That we did not need armor,
or steel, or cannon.
We just need each other.

He spoke to us about brotherhood,
about lines of men who live together,
eat together, train together,
fight and die together.

That we were joining the absolute illustrious
history of the Furious First.
1st War Machine, 1st Regiment,
1st Battalion. Infantry.

Since the formation of the War Machines,
and their Warships that scour the stars,
purging Xenos from planets,
or being decimated by alien armadas,

the 1st War Machine has endured,
rooted deep into the fight for Mankind.
With its nine Regiments and the Hero of Humanity,
the first Juggernaught.

In the Original Regiment, with its
three Battalions of men,
I was assigned to the Furious First,
numerically number one,

which was a fine, cohesive group.
Training began immediately,
my squad happening to be in Alpha Company,
the fiercest Company in the Battalion. Told to run,

and run we did. We ran hills,
we ran fields, we ran with packs,
we ran with no armor. We ran to the range,
where I quickly learned my rifle.

I found out I was a natural,
or at least that's what the marksmen called me,
and so I was appointed as point man,
the soldier in front of the whole squad.

The point man of 1st squad.
I was first in everything,
first to be done in battle class,
first to finish my meal. To hit the rack.

First to step off the droppod,
us being fired into the writhing pit,
the Xenos swarming immediately.
Pulling my squadmates apart.

The rifles we've been armed with
weren't necessarily weak.
For a single man to have in his hands,
it was a large amount of power.

A Xenos monster,
with its greenish, thick skin,
stood seven feet tall,
muscle bound, clawed.

They needed a large caliber
to break them down,
and the rifle delivered.
Ninety rounds of thick fury.

Underslung the barrel,
a tube launcher, breech loaded,
popped off grenades to end the Xenos,
the green hulks, the scourge.

In this moment I thought of the blur of training,
the countless runs,
the fire talks of Man
and what we stand for.

We stand for the fighting spirit of Humanity,
the ferocity of thousands of years
of the warring species
and all its pent up energy.

Infantry. The backbone of the War Machine,
my drowsiness gone. The squad I belong to
and I pushed out the droppod,
blazing our rifles and popping off grenades,

the enemy being ripped to shreds.
Our squad being pulled apart.
A scream opened up from the sky,
and artillery fire poured down like rain.

No armor or Bipedals were in sight,
so we fought up the slight hill
to get to higher ground,
any advantage a substantial one.

The truth was that we had to make up
for our shortcomings.
Rifle ammo and grenades
only did so much.

We had to be aggressive,
and smart. We had to be
moving, forward, pushing,
and never slowing down.

We never slowed down. My first campaign ended,
my kills started with memories,
but then turned to a number.
We never seemed to sleep.

Campaign after campaign,
leading new troops as their point men,
I fought the Xenos with a human fury,
feats of bravery were my common ploy.

Then came one battle,
after a year of waging war,
in a unit I would never have wished
to not be a part of.

In this battle, we were on a purple planet,
it's landscape so alien
like the aliens we were killing.
The battle wasn't going well.

Another aspect of Infantry,
Heavy Weapons Company, or Heavies,
opened up all over.
The Machine Gun crews lining up.

These groups would drop their tripods
and mount their massive auto-guns
on the fly, laying waste
or laying cover fire.

Shoulder mounted,
hydraulic-frame supported hand cannons
were walked into place, firing high-angle
mortars to bombard close enemy.

Teams of launchers, two per,
spaced themselves around Alpha Company,
spearing rockets and missiles
into enemy armor or formations.

The mix of our Company's offensive,
Beta Company's feign to the right
and the Heavies of Comna Company suppression
led my squad's path to the very front.

To stop was certain death,
and so here we were,
the mighty versus the meek,
the Xenos against Man.

Soon I found myself face-to-face
with a snarling green mug.
His head was twice mine,
his shoulders as broad as my arm span.

Its own rifle too large for me to handle,
or any human for that matter,
as it bore down to end me.
This was it.

A split second of defeat,
was soundly defeated by my will.
I will not fall!
Never!

I am the first son in my family!
I am the first man on the ground!
I am of the Furious First!
I am first to fight!

First to kill.
First to die.
And that's what I did,
my last thoughts

as I was pulled into halves.
My last action,
to die.
To pull the trigger

of the launcher
that found itself
underneath the chin
of the Xenos.

First to kill!"

*As an artilleryman, I have a love for all ground forces. Tanks, Infantry,*
*Artillery. I have a lot of 0311 friends and enjoy their company. This piece was*
*trying to grasp that.*

# 97 CONVEYANCE

"I'm real,
I'm real as you feel.
I feel for you,
tell me who else would do all this

for you.
The act, the trial
of treating words
as colossal themes

in our effort to push ideas,
feelings and emotions out
is astounding. Believe,
look around you, up at the clouds.

The spin, or fly,
or blow over, whatever the scientific term,
as is what they should do.
Precipitation ensues,

condensation before,
a number of other large words
and it's a cycle we can see.
Because we've seen it.

So, in the same line of thinking,
are things limited to what we experience
that we can write about?
Think, do I need to know love

to write about love?
I can write about love,
I do often.
About the most minute detail

of what it means
to be in love.
To brush your hair
past your ears to which

you can lock your lips
tight with mine,
my own heart fluttering to match
the tempo of the night.

Or day, or morning,
the way I wake with the sun
pouring into the room,
the blinds closed tight

from the night before,
the pillows and comforter
on the floor
from before, waking up.

Next to the one I love,
or loved. Only now can I write
about the time with her,
but have I conveyed that love?

No,
not even close.
So there's the dilemma,
the idea of communication done right.

Accurate,
but using a plethora
of words found in a thesaurus
isn't the recipe for perfect writing.

Who determines perfect writing.
You do. Yes, you,
and the person in front of me,
the girl to my left,
also you,

the couple in front of us,
us being both poet and another person
with her own life, phone,
dreams and conveyance of life.

Writing about life,
for me,
isn't about painting the perfect picture.
It's about painting you a picture.

Each poem,
a different artwork
for every canvas that opens up to it,
every mind that thinks my words through.

Some paintings are hazy,
full of blotches and carelessness,
others are emotional,
phenomenal art.

Art is what we see,
it's how we decorate our life.
Art, decorating space.
Music, decorating time.

Poetry,
decorating minds.
Have I conveyed that?
Do you see what I see?

I don't know.
But think about the life
we all share,
all breathe together.

That is the point,
as a race. To share,
as a people. In others words,
to listen. To care."

# 98 THE INSOMNIACS

"Bastard children.
Forgotten.
We are the unglorified,
the unappreciated.

We are the taxis,
the transporters. The bombers,
the drop-podders and guntoters,
the fly-highers.

The liars, the easy-lifers,
the ones that are hated.

We are the Air Wing.

And we love our life.

The beginning of Basic Course
has an immediate division
between those destined to be ground pounders
and the men of the sky.

That was the only choice you made
as you turned twenty and went to train.
Whether you would join the multitude of men
that were going to be killed planetside

or, instead, you would find the glory
of piloting the highly sophisticated,
magnificent machines of the Air Wing.
They had no equal.

That was our opinion, and it was right.
Tanks? Bipedals? They are ants,
and we are the birds of prey.
We are the best.

It pays to be the best,
for we had an easy life.
Or so we thought, considering
that was what was advertised.

Clean machines,
once we finished the grueling process
of the Basic Course with those mongrels
and left on the skids to the airfields

we all broke out in smiles.
We had made it, we were away
from those who always spoke sour,
unbeknownst to our future power.

Power indeed,
the feed of brass and metal
into all of our guns
made us the most lethal.

Arrogance? Nay,
confidence.
We fly, they die.
That was our motto.

Every War Machine had Air Wings,
one for killing,
one for moving.
The moving?

They were lacking,
they're only purpose to deploy
the ground pounders. Though,
it was sort of a sight to behold

when a War Machine went to fight.
Seeing a squadron of Magpads
trawl a battalion of tanks planetside
was like watching a swarm of bees.

Even better was the bigger Magpads
that dropped the Bipedals.
They would fly so low and let loose
the walking hounds from tens of feet above.

They would then land and pounce,
or prowl, or whatever they called it.
They were the only ones worth mentioning.
Well, scratch that,

that one big Bipedal was impressive,
some sort of sacred Hero.
Though, we rarely see Him.
He gets dropped straight from the Warship.

Drop-podders were inspiring.
The Companies of troops would load
up into huge Dropships.
They had three pods inside,

and once a War Machine was deployed,
after the armor were flown in
peppering the Xenos with Air-to-Ground Missiles,
or was we pronounced, 'ah-gums',

the giant Dropships skirting low orbit
would position and then drop whole squads,
firing from its belly
droppods explosively into the battle.

The Dropships, delivering the load
of Man and their machines to lay waste
and death. Magpads buzzing in,
followed by searing clumps of droppods.

Designed to literally blow up,
the droppods would scream down into the enemy,
like rounds from the far-off Cracken Cannons,
and before any smoke had cleared,

the Xenos would have upon them
a pack of wild dogs, the Infantry
of the War Machine. Aided by the threat
of the treaded Tank,

the metal of the lumbering
Bipedal, and the long medley
of the far-reaching Artillery.
All ground pounders.

But eventually,
after the Air Wing of Dropships left station,
and the Xenos started to turn the tide,
we would be deployed.

The Air Wing of Fear.
The true threat to the Xenos.
We would fall onto them,
and destroy them.

Back when we would begin training,
we would learn to train at night.
The need for sleep would never be erased,
but we learned to stay up when we shouldn't.

It wasn't that we weren't afforded
the opportunity to sleep,
but we just couldn't. At night,
we'd all be wide awake.

And that's what lent us our nickname,
the Night Fighters,
though the idea was a bit thoughtless.
There was a lack of day-and-night cycle

in space.
The Warship made its own with dimming lights
and announcement of 'lights out'.
But we never listened. We were above

the sleep-chained ground pounders.
Chained, however, we were
to this damnable boat called a Warship.
A primate could pilot it.

Unlike what we had in our Air Wing.
The 8th Air Wing had three Groups,
like any other regiment in the 1st War Machine.
But each had its own specialty.

The 9th Air Wing was the same way,
each Dropship Group responsible
for deploying either troops,
tanks or Bipedals specifically.

But we had the real fighters.
The air-to-air combat flyers.
The dogs of the air.
And life was good.

1st Group had Gunships,
the buzzing hornets of the Wing.
Low altitude were their specialty,
and a Squadron of these

could spare a Company of troops
a fate of being dismembered.
Or a Band of Bipedals
a fate of crushing flame.

3rd Group had Bombers,
two Squadrons of fast, light bombers
with these swiveling, manually aimed
protective machine guns.

One Squadron of the 3rd were huge,
large bombers with four gun turrets
and hundreds of bombs that would be dropped
on the Xenos with devastating effect.

But the 2nd?
We were the glorious,
finest sons of Man,
nothing could match us.

The Xenos had some wild gear,
and for the most part,
would give the ground pounders
a very hard time.

In the stars, Armadas were evenly matched,
space battles always turning into a stalemate.
The Fleets of Mans Battleships, Dragoons
and swarming Carriers never seemed to crush.

A battle for a planet,
strategic or otherwise,
was rarely finished in space only.
The Fleets of Man hitting walls.

They would engage in ship-to-ship battle,
but after no upper hand,
the Warship that was holding back
would move up and deploy its terrible cargo.

And so the fight would move planetside,
the Xenos pouring out of,
well,
whatever they use.

But the whole time, we would be deployed.
The single-manned space fighters,
able to jump in and out of orbit,
to slice and dice the Cruisers of the Xenos.

The main point of our Group
was to protect the Warship,
to swathe through the oncoming,
cumbersome, heavy ships

the Xenos would launch to thwart
our vessel as it bears over the ongoing campaign.
The Battleships, quite ugly looking,
would keep the large Xenos Maneater ships at bay.

The only ones to slip were the smaller Cruisers,
who by comparison were three times our Fighters,
but we made up for size with numbers,
and skill. We were deadly.

That's where we came alive.
Unable to sleep the whole time,
space blurring what point of the day it was,
or night,

we would shoot out of the Warship
like darts out of a tube,
thrusters searing behind as we launched
towards the Cruisers.

All the simulation in the galaxy
could not prepare a pilot
for the ferocity of fighter combat.
It was an intense ordeal.

Each Fighter armed with machine guns
for line-of-sight offense,
missiles for a more definitive
end to the conversation.

These tools, combined with our skills
to delicately tear about space
is what makes us the absolute best.
The ground pounders were nothing.

So here we were,
apparently it was night time,
but I was wide awake,
as if it was midday.

The latest campaign ensuing,
2nd Group of the 8th Air Wing
busting out into space
to protect and surge the Xenos away.

Leading the Squadron forward,
a line of Fighters,
looking like magnificent flying raptors,
sped in perfect formation,

breaking off into a spiral of ships
going all over the place
as soon as the Xenos were in
weapon range.

The fight had begun,
tracer rounds zipping all over,
but muffled, as there was
no atmosphere in space for sound to move about.

A Cruiser was to my bottom left,
I dived down and spun completely around
in one movement, now
behind the slow Cruiser.

I squeeze the trigger key
and let loose a missile screaming
to the hulk in front,
watch it be torn apart by unforgiving space.

Here, we tore them apart,
instead of the Xenos ripping
troops into pieces.
We made the fight even.

A Cruiser got lucky,
shooting their huge guns
and lighting a Fighter
into a fiery, silent explosion.

We made it pay,
two Fighters swooping in from
either side. Time to die,
and the Cruiser did under machine gun fire.

The rest of the Squadron
were mopping up,
but before we could regroup
six of us were immediately destroyed.

Surprised, comm chatter going nuts,
we soon realized a large Xenos Maneater
slipped past our Battleships and Dragoons,
and now was steaming towards our Warship.

We could not lose the Warship,
for every Man planetside would be doomed.
Besides the fact
we would have nowhere to rest.

So we swarmed,
every Fighter letting loose fury
at the Maneater,
a fearsome spaceship that matched the Battleship in size.

Its main cannon
had opened its muzzle,
a gaping hole
pointed right at our home.

I swooped down,
restless,
and spun upside down
into the barrel of the gigantic weapon.

I had so little room,
but I wasn't worried.
Because I was already blasting my forward thrusters,
blasting straight backwards.

Exiting the gaping cannon,
and zipping straight up,
but not before firing
every single missile I had on deck.

The missiles flow deep down,
and I screamed in the comm
for every Fighter to bug out,
there was about to be a show.

The Maneater ship burst,
from the middle a crack split its side,
before being devoured in a horrible explosion.
Horrible for the Xenos.

The threat thwarted,
we left to spin around and swipe oncoming Cruisers.
We were unstoppable.
We were the best.

I zoomed back towards the Warship,
it slowing down before I saw
from beneath its belly
a giant droppod fire down to the planet.

I guess the big Bipedal was deployed,
but no matter.
It had nothing on the Air Wing.
The finest sons of Men.

At least,
that's what we told ourselves,
when we were wide awake at night.
Sleep was for the weak."

*My imagined perspective of the Air Wing. Cockiness and confidence coincides so well.*

# 99 THE COUNCIL

"Barred,
but undeterred,
the fact of the matter is,
I wanted to come inside.

Invited to the building,
of height and yellow,
across from the fellows
who jovially drank the burn.

But I,
dry as ever,
was sweating the night away,
having pushed up the Georgian hill.

Arrived, was I,
but unable to enter.
The door was closed shut,
and the occupants?

Meditating,
perhaps intensely,
communication unable to share
the immense feelings upstairs.

Unbeknownst to me,
of course,
the one stuck outside,
staring into the glass door,

doors shut tight
like a seal from the outside.
Sealing the world, humid,
off from the cold dry air.

Without a care,
I tried every one,
but my efforts led to no solution,
realization I may have to leave.

Indeed,
outside for a time,
my purpose was empty
so the look was to the end of the street.

And then my left
filled with motion,
a woman leaving the building,
and an opportunity presented.

So now I pounced,
brushing through past the woman,
who had me observed intensely,
my purpose now shady.

To her.
To me, still lost,
the next door locked,
but the directory had a number,

053, and it rang,
for too many tones perhaps,
the woman outside steady staring,
a furrowed brow on me.

But before I was interrogated,
the buzzer sounded loud,
and I was let into the atrium
and made my way upstairs.

The fifth floor was there,
up long flights of stairs,
as I approached the smell
of an apartment full of people.

And the entrance?
Wow, so warm,
the room full of people
so absolute inviting.

So I sat,
at this Council of the Moon,
totally enthused with the subject,
and observant of their love.

They interacted slowly,
with a familiar love that warmed my skin,
as the Sun kisses me all over,
they washed me in light.

But the light was from within,
their Inner Light bright,
reflecting the outer light
off their inner Moon.

So I sat, and we talked,
sharing deep stories and trials,
with people I barely knew,
yet who were so open with me.

We spoke about me,
attentions turned to me,
and the opportunity
afforded to me

to be there for a friend,
and they all sighed in admiration.
Such love! This Council
poured unto me.

It was nice to speak out
our intentions soon to come,
but, all the while,
observing all members

and loving every second.
The second it ended,
some left,
while the rest sat around,

and they listened to my written word.
One of them almost had me,
the Marine, with eyes wet.
Bet, it was touching

to have such praise.
A fellow poet, spat spoken,
sharing her old poem 'If',
a work of art itself.

So here is the end,
the trial coming to a close.
These people,
giving unto me,

the indication that my poems
are more than mediocre.
Reader,
what do you say?

Let the Council decide.
Am I a poet?
Am I one with my soul?

Yes."

# 100 THE HARDEST THING I'VE EVER WRITTEN, OR, THE WILDCAT'S CUB

"A Child was born.
To Him, poetry was
dedicated to. Rounds,
artillery, were fired for.

The Sun rose,
Experiment 626 resided with,
Manolo was gifted,
the Earth turned.

The Ocean ebbed,
as it always does,
and things that always happen,
happened.

In a room,
so immensely packed with support,
love,
cherished, sweet love,

a Son was born.
A Son was graced into the world,
the exact moment a blur of imagination.
And tears fell for the glory of life's gift.

The gift to make life,
the gift to give love to one another,
and to always be there.
No other way, really.

In this room,
Mother and Father,
two sets were there,
watched what their children's actions

brought to be.
A beautiful moment,
and from the Woman,
having had her heart gone through much,

having had loss and gain,
was a strength in the room
that made it all come together
into one point of joy and tears.

Tears of joy,
a happy sob
fell from the Man
who watched his Son being born.

This Man,
one wearing the colors of the Woman's tribe,
had shared an intimate moment
with the one giving birth,

and sat in awe
at the Son that was born.
The Man became a Father,
and that is where I frown.

For I was not that Man.

I was not the one in the room,
watching his Son be born.

I was not the one holding the hand
of the Woman I loved.

I was not a part of the moment
that I had to imagine to
write so acutely about.

Instead,
the dust of the desert,
a home to Her,
and Hell for me,

was the terrain I slept in,
constantly thinking
of the Woman and the
Child that was born.

Every day it was the same thing.
I paid what I had, and had nothing left,
I clock in, I clock out.
I grab the wrench, and turn the bolt.

The dirt encrusted Kevlar
that kept my matted hair flat
was so distracting,
but not so much that

I hadn't spent every single second
dreaming of the Son that wasn't mine.
That never was going to be,
but I wanted Him to be.

Oh, Lord,
I had to get away,
and away I did when I finally made it.
Finally

out of the desert,
supposedly the very last time,
washing truck, howitzer,
uniform, flack,

body, face,
mind, and soul.
The shower drain struggled,
the surfboard over waxed.

And finally,
after being asked,
I got into the one called Alice,
a name the Woman and I even spoke about

for children of our own,
and sped far from Base,
to the City that I loved,
to the Woman who had broken up

with me, yet we were still
deep in love.
Always have been.
And walking in,

bending over to pet the Puggle
that I so affectionately looked after,
the Woman stood in the doorway,
a surprise in her arms.

Asleep, was He,
I hadn't even gotten a look. She put the Child
down, into the crib I had built
with my own hands.

We leaned over together,
staring at the little angel
like a Mother and Father
look at their Son.

But before the anger
of the Jealousy I had
for the Man who was really the Father
could swell up my throat,

the Wildcat and I embraced,
the first time being so close
since Gas Lamp rendezvous,
full of drunken kisses and black outs,

which was replaced with a relationship
that from the start we knew
was difficult,
considering the baby in between.

Did that stop us?
No, just gave me an excuse
to live out my desire
to be a father.

A father, but not the Father.
Yet, was the Man there to comfort Her?
To be there for Her
when she was tired, sad, and hungry?

No, it was me,
making every meal a feast,
a gourmet entree,
or at least that's what I tried.

And She obliged,
cringing at the Mustard Seed
but smiling at the effort.
An effort unfailingly

putting up with her worries,
putting up with her wrath,
putting up shelves with skill.
Well, and I had a drill.

And the will,
driving once at 0300,
to be there at 0400,
to spend an hour until 0500,

before showing up to formation,
holding her in my arms,
kissing her belly,
living a life that wasn't mine.

Seething Jealousy hit me,
eventually,
when I realized the Man
was the Father. Not me.

Yet,
I teared up
when I held the Son,
with an age of six days,

for the very first time,
and sang sweet songs to him,
from First Light, to Bad Seeds,
and His Mothers favorite, Jack.

A lack
of attention to the time,
the all-of-a-sudden affection
and the kisses that made us a couple again.

I had spent nights
rubbing Her softly,
like I had written before,
palm flat against the life inside.

And now, here He was.
In my arms.
All the while,
so much doubt

from so many folks
who looked down at me, though
size wasn't the issue. I wasn't
short on stature, just age.

Among other things,
and the lack of feelings
and the experience of handling
such a Jealousy

lead me to hide a contempt
for a person I hadn't even met.
Over what?
A Son that wasn't even mine.

Every second with the Child
had me torn.
The fact of the matter was,
I loved Him before he was born.

Justified? Not at all,
as I pulled on my black hat.
A gift, eventually meant
for the Cub of the Wildcat.

But will He where it?
Will He want it?
A gift from a Boy
who held Him close?

Goodness gracious,
I'm sorry
I'm so crazy.
I'm sorry..."

*A confession.*

# ABOUT THE AUTHOR

Donovan Blaze Walters is a poet who happens to be many other things; a jack of all trades, a master of none. Having lived all over the States, he claims California, though really from Washington. He currently lives and writes in Tennessee while performing his duties as an Artillery Mechanic in the United States Marine Corps.

24482890R00195

Made in the USA
Middletown, DE
27 September 2015